.99

1989

Love Martin. x

Thomas Hardy

A Life in Pictures

Jo Draper

THE DOVECOTE PRESS

First published in 1989 by
The Dovecote Press Ltd
Stanbridge, Wimborne, Dorset BH21 4JD

ISBN 0 946159 71 8

© Jo Draper 1989

Designed by Humphrey Stone
Typeset in Palatino by Character Graphics,
Taunton, Somerset
Printed and bound by Biddles Ltd,
Guildford and King's Lynn

Contents

Acknowledgements

In 1906 Hardy wrote to Leslie Stephen's biographer, 'A man of letters should be set before the world in a literary manner'. I can only hope that Hardy would not have minded being set forth before the world in photographs. Hardy did object to the 'quizzing impertinence' of remarks 'on one's appearance, clothing, household details, etc', but in 1914 he wrote to a friend 'I do not, on truth feel *much* interest in posthumous opinions about me, or estimates and shall sleep quite calmly at Stinsford whatever happens'.

As always I am grateful to the staff of the Dorset County Library (Lending and Reference) for all their help; to Sheena Pearce for word-processing and to Christopher Chaplin for the maps and to my mother for her help. I am grateful to Mr and Mrs T.W. Jesty for answering queries, and to Roger Peers of the Dorset County Museum for permission to use so much material from the Hardy and general collections.

All unattributed quotations in the text are from *The Life of Thomas Hardy* published as being by Florence Hardy, but largely written by Hardy himself. Some of the letters quoted are from that publication, but most from *The Collected Letters of Thomas Hardy* edited by Richard Little Purdy and Michael Millgate (Oxford University Press, seven volumes 1978-1988).

I am grateful to the following for permission to use illustrations. To Columbia Picture Industries Inc for the photographs on p. 85 (bottom) and p. 124. To the Dorset County Library, Dorchester for p. 30, p. 31 (top), p. 37, p. 114 (top), p. 117 (top), and p. 122 (both at top). To The Dorset Natural History and Archaeological Society, Dorset County Museum, Dorchester, for the photographs on p. 13, p. 106 (top) and p. 112 (bottom) from the Hansford Collection; on p. 43 (right) from the Barnes Collection; on p. 119 from the Hardy Collection; and on p. 11 (top), p. 20 (bottom), p. 27, p. 29 (top), p. 40, p. 41, p. 42, p. 45 (both), p. 46 (top), p. 56 (bottom), p. 58 (top), p. 69, p. 70, p. 71 (both), p. 74 (bottom two), p. 75 (top), p. 79, p. 80 (top), and p. 92 (bottom), and p. 104 (top) from the Photographic Record. Fay Godwin for the photograph on p. 19. The Howarth-Loomes Collection, the photographs on p. 52 and 53. Mr and Mrs T.W. Jesty for the photographs on p. 22 (top and left). Antony Kersting Esq. for the photographs on p. 14, p. 34, p. 63 and p. 74 (top). H.E.F. Lock for permission to use photographs from the Lock Collection, Dorset County Library for p. 18 (middle), p. 54 (bottom), p. 84 (top), p. 94 (bottom), p. 97 (top right); p. 97 (bottom), p. 106 (bottom), and p. 122 (bottom). Museum of Rural Life, Reading for p. 75 (bottom). The National Monuments Record for p. 51 and p. 54 (top) and for prints of the Howarth-Loomes photographs. The National Trust for p. 18 (top). The Rector and churchwardens of St Julietta's church, St Juliot, Cornwall for permission to use p. 59, both photographs. The Royal Library. Windsor, for p. 101 (left). The Syndics of the Fitzwilliam Museum

Cambridge for p. 107. The Trustees of the Thomas Hardy Memorial Collection in the Dorset County Museum, Dorchester, Dorset, for the photographs on the frontispiece; p. 11 (bottom), p. 12, p. 17, p. 20 (top), p. 21, p. 22 (right), p. 23, p. 24 (top), p. 24 (bottom), p. 28 (all three), p. 29 (bottom left and right), p. 31 (bottom), p. 33 (both), p. 36, p. 38, p. 43 (left) p. 44, p. 46 (bottom), p. 47, p. 50 (both), p. 55 (all three), p. 56 (top), p. 57, p. 58 (bottom), p. 60 (both), p. 61 (both), p. 64, p. 67, p. 72 (both), p. 78, p. 80 (bottom), p. 81, p. 82, p. 85 (top), p. 86 (top), p. 87, p. 88, p. 90, p. 91 (both), p. 92 (top), p. 94 (top), p. 95, p. 96 (both), p. 97 (top left), p. 98 (both, p. 99, p. 100 (all three), p. 101 (top and bottom right), p. 104 (bottom), p. 105, p. 108 (both), p. 109, p. 110 (both), p. 111 (both), p. 112 (top), p. 114 (bottom), p. 116, p. 117 (bottom), p. 118, p. 119 (top), p. 120 and p. 121 (both). To Warner Brothers Distributors Ltd for the photographs on p. 68 (bottom) and p. 123.

Dorchester and Bockhampton in the 1880s

R. Piddle

PUDDLETOWN

HEATHLAND

Hardy's Birthplace

HIGHER BOCKHAMPTON

DORCHESTER

STINSFORD

Kingston
Maurwood
House

LOWER BOCKHAMPTON

School

FORDINGTON

Path

Path

WATER   MEADOWS

R. Frome

Max Gate

Talbothays

Barnes'
Rectory

Railway

0   1   2

MILES

WINTERBORNE CAME   WHITCOMBE

Introduction

Photography and Thomas Hardy were born at much the same time, so there are photographs of him all through his life, starting with one of the shy youth of sixteen and ending with later photographs means that the image of the old man tends to blot out the far more vigorous looking, bearded younger one who was the novelist. The series of portraits gives a far better idea of the man than any description can, and there are also photographs of the people he knew, the houses he lived in and the landscape in which he set his novels and poetry.

Although Hardy sketched all his life, he did not take photographs and disliked being 'Kodaked' by trippers. He also refused to be filmed 'moving' in 1922 by a film company who were shooting *Tess* partly in Dorchester. After he had stopped writing fiction he enjoyed many trips with a photographer friend who was illustrating '*Thomas Hardy's Wessex*,' and like many other people he collected photographs of friends and places he had visited. His collection included a few of the places he had written about as well.

All these illustrations help us to see Hardy and his life more clearly. The contrast between the cottage he was born in and the house he built himself is difficult to explain fully, but easily appreciated from photographs. The landscapes he loved are even more difficult to define in words, but are clear from pictures.

In his long lifetime Hardy had three careers. For the first thirty years he was educated and became an architect's assistant. For the next twenty-five years he wrote fiction, and for his last thirty-three years he returned to poetry, his first love. He was born into the working classes, lived most of his life as one of the middle class, but earned as much money as the upper classes.

Although firmly associated with the Wessex of his novels and poems, especially his native Dorset, he lived in London for five years as a young man, and called himself almost half a Londoner. When young he wanted to become a clergyman, but from middle age he was a famous agnostic. Hardy is full of contradictions and enigmas: a reserved, elusive man who wrote revealing poetry. No-one has ever satisfactorily answered Gosse's famous question 'What has Providence done to Mr Hardy, that he should rise up in the arable land of Wessex and shake his fist at his Creator?'

Parts of the answer might have been found in Hardy's personal papers, destroyed by him or his second wife. Little is known of his life in London as a young man, or of his emotional life before he met his first wife. However, much of his life is in his fiction and poetry, although interpretation is tantalisingly difficult. This is not to say that the characters in his novels are portraits, or that all the poetry is autobiographical. Hardy despised what he called 'slice of life' fiction: in his speech accepting the freedom of his native borough of Dorchester in 1910 he defended *The Mayor of Casterbridge*. 'At any rate, it is not a photograph in words, that inartistic species of literary produce, particularly in respect of personages'.

The difficulty is in Hardy's realistic settings – because his birthplace is used as the setting for *Under the Greenwood Tree* we can easily imagine that the family represented is his. When he describes a courtship in Cornwall at the very time he is courting there, we assume that the architect hero is himself, and so on. This is not true: of course a novelist (especially in early books) must draw on his own character when writing, but Hardy's characters are inventions of his imagination. They reveal a good deal about the writer, and sometimes odd characteristics and events are based on real ones, but it is a mistake to think that Jude is Hardy, or Sue Bridehead Mrs Hardy.

Given that the characters are invented, we can see much of Hardy's life in their settings. These are always observations (although altered to suit the plot or mood of the book), and even his honeymoon (and first trip abroad) is used.

Some of the poetry is clearly autobiographical and strongly emotional. Hardy claimed in a letter of 1919 that there was 'more autobiography in a hundred lines of Mr Hardy's poetry than in all the novels'. The outpouring of poems about his first wife Emma after her death is the clearest example, but throughout the whole of the poetry there are personal poems, nakedly reflecting Hardy's attitudes, and reactions, indeed all his emotions.

One tends to identify Hardy the man with his writings, especially the sad or traumatic parts of his novels and the deeply felt poetry, making him into a tragic person. In fact he was a full-time writer from the age of 32, a successful one from a couple of years after that, and even in his childhood his parents had enough money to send him to a good school and to have him trained as an architect. One of the last notes he wrote in 1927, sounding a little odd as he writes about himself as 'H', shows that he appreciated this. 'It must not be forgotten that H's own life and experiences had been smoother and happier than many – perhaps the majority. It was his habit, or *strange* power of putting himself in the place of those who endured sufferings from which he himself had been in the main free, or subject to but at brief times.' This may have been written to cheer his second wife, but is probably a reasonable epitaph.

Opposite top. Hardy's birthplace, the cottage at Higher Bockhampton, near Dorchester where he lived until he was twenty-one and where his parents lived all their lives. Probably taken about 1900, when Hardy's mother, sisters and brother were still there.

Opposite bottom. Max Gate, the house Hardy designed for himself in the early 1880s, and built only a couple of miles from his birthplace, photographed in 1919. He lived here for forty-three years.

12

Hardy the novelist, and the poet. Left in about 1890, aged fifty, the time he was
writing *Tess of the D'Urbervilles*; and above aged eighty-four in 1924.   13

One of Hardy's favourite views, from Pilsdon Pen in West Dorset, one of the hills in his poem 'Wessex Heights'.

His Grandparents and the Past

The Thomas Hardy born in 1840 was the third of that name, and the third generation to live in the thatched cob cottage at Higher Bockhampton. The setting was romantic, on the boundary of heath and woodlands, remote yet only a couple of miles (easy walking distance) from Dorset's county town, Dorchester.

Dorset in 1840 was an isolated and backward county, still completely agricultural, with no industry to compete for labour, and the agricultural labourers (the bulk of the population) were paid only enough for bare subsistence. Higher Bockhampton was one of several scattered hamlets which made up the small village of Stinsford.

The cottage was built by his great grandfather at the end of a lane leading onto a heath, and was isolated enough to be used in Hardy's grandfather's time as a smugglers' store. From 1801-5 up to eighty barrels of brandy were stored in the house, and Hardy recorded in his notebook that one of the little elongated barrels survived in his time 'turned into a bucket by knocking out one head, and putting [on] a handle'.

Thomas Hardy the first, the novelist's grandfather, was the first to live there, moving into the cottage in 1801. He was dead before the novelist was born, but his widow Mary lived there with the family until her death in 1857. Hardy's first surviving poem 'Domicilium', written three or four years later, recounts her stories of the cottage soon after it was built fifty years before:

> 'Our house stood quite alone, and those tall firs
> And beeches were not planted. Snakes and efts
> Swarmed in the summer days, and nightly bats
> Would fly about our bedrooms. Heath-croppers
> Lived on the hills, and were our only friends:
> So wild it was when first we settled here.'

Mary Hardy came from Fawley in Berkshire, later used by Hardy as the setting for part of *Jude*, where she was orphaned and had an unhappy childhood. Although not Dorset born she lived at Bockhampton for almost sixty years, providing part of that continuity with the past in one small area which Hardy later valued so much. He knew that mobility 'led to a break in continuity in local history, more fatal than any other thing to the preservation of legend, folklore, close inter-social relations, and eccentric individualities. For these the indispensable conditions of existence are attachment to the soil of one particular spot by generation after generation' (introduction to *Far from the Madding Crowd*).

The poem 'One we knew' (M. H. 1772–1857), written almost fifty years after his grandmother's death, includes some of the scenes she brought alive for him:

'She showed us the spot where the
      maypole was yearly planted,
  And where the bandsmen stood
While breeched and kerchiefed partners
      whirled, and panted
  To choose each other for good.
With cap-framed face and long gaze into
      the embers –
  We seated around her knees –
She would dwell on such dead themes,
      not as one who remembers,
  But rather as one who sees.'

Hardy believed that his family had come down in the world, and that most of his ancestors, paternal or maternal, were once higher in the social scale. This probably wasn't true, but the truth is much less important than what Hardy believed. He thought the family descended from the le Hardys from Jersey, and 'often thought he would like to restore the "le" to his name . . . but never did so.' The Hardy family in this time 'had all the characteristics of an old family of spent social energies'. He was careful only to say that the Elizabethan Thomas Hardy who founded the grammar school in Dorchester and Admiral Sir Thomas Masterman Hardy of Trafalgar fame, were one of the 'diverse Dorset sections' of the Hardy family, as no link between them and the novelist's family could ever be made.

Hardy used the idea of decayed families in almost all his fiction, most notably in *Jude* and *Tess*. Tess's whole life is altered by events which occur because she is remotely descended from the knightly D'Urbervilles, although her family had adapted the name to the more homely Durbeyfield.

Knowledge of Bockhampton – both the place and its people – before his birth was important to Hardy, coming out in many poems, *The Trumpet Major*, and his verse drama *The Dynasts*, both set at the time of the Napoleonic Wars. He consciously used much true rural detail, like folklore, in all his works: his nostalgia for the recent past, fuelled by his grandparent's memories, comes over clearly in his prose and poetry.

Caption overleaf

Slyer's Lane Lime Kiln,

Within a Mile and Half of Dorchester.

The Public are respectfully informed that they can be supplied with good well-burnt

LIME

At the above Kiln, at the undermentioned prices, viz.

At the Kiln, ... **1s. 8d.** per Sack.

Delivered, ... **2s. 0d.** ditto.

All orders directed to Mr. Thomas Hardy, at the Post-Office, Dorchester, or to George Downton, at the Kiln, will be strictly attended to.

Dated February, 1825

Previous page. The cottage, Higher Bockhampton, built by Hardy's great-grandfather for his son, drawn by Hardy the novelist. The family rented the land, with the lease falling in at the death of the named life-holders, when it and the cottage reverted to the landowner. Called copyhold, this was a common form of tenure, used dramatically by Hardy in several novels including *The Woodlanders* and *Tess of the D'Urbervilles*.

Above. Inside Hardy's birthplace, Higher Bockhampton. Hardy described it as a 'seven-roomed rambling house', but really it is only a decent sized Dorset cottage. He wrote *Under the Greenwood Tree* and *Far from the Madding Crowd* upstairs in this room, helped his father in the autumn with the cider making, and was generally involved in the rural life he was writing about.

Left. Hardy's grandfather advertising lime in 1825, part of his mason's business. Hardy wrote in 1881: 'From time immemorial – I can speak from certain knowledge of four generations – my direct ancestors have all been master-masons, with a set of journeymen masons under them. Though they have never risen above this level, they have *never* sunk below it . . .'. Hardy may have slightly exaggerated here: his forbears were probably not always employers, but they were certainly independent craftsmen.

Right. The back of the cottage at Higher Bockhampton, a modern photograph by Fay Godwin which gives the atmosphere of its woodland setting, and the simplicity of its thatch and cob.

Left. A more distant view of the cottage, Higher Bockhampton taken about 1900, clearly showing the heathland behind. Higher Bockhampton and the other scattered hamlets made up the village of Stinsford which had less than 400 inhabitants in 1841, the year after Hardy was born.

Lower left. The footpath along the river from Stinsford to Dorchester, a favourite walk of Hardy's all his life. The rich watermeadows contrast with the nearby heathlands, something Hardy emphasises in *The Return of the Native* and *Tess*. Dorchester, the county town of Dorset, is just visible background left.

The Dynasts Hardy's poetic drama set in Napoleonic time, bringing to life the time of his grandparents, was adapted and shortened as a 'patriotic drama' in 1914 after the First World War had started, and professionally produced in London. In the introduction to *The Trumpet Major* Hardy recalled the 'casual relics' of the Napoleonic period which still existed in Dorset up to the middle of the 19th century, which 'brought to my imagination in early childhood the state of affairs at the date of the war more vividly than volumes of history could have done'. In a cupboard at the cottage he found contemporary periodicals bought by his grandfather 'with their melodramatic prints of serried ranks, crossed bayonets, huge knapsacks, and dead bodies'.

Opposite top. Hardy's novel *The Trumpet Major* adapted for the stage and performed by The Hardy Players in 1908, in the Corn Exchange, Dorchester. Hardy told a correspondent that one of the special attributes of this production was the fact that 'the grandparents of the actors (many of them) were the real actors in more or less the scenes depicted – that they know all the events traditionally'. Real pikes and guns were used, local survivals.

Far left. Miss E. Hawker as Anne Garland in the 1912 revival of the Hardy Players' production of *The Trumpet Major*.

Left. A jug decorated with prints ridiculing Napoleon bought by Hardy. These were made in great quantities during the Napoleonic Wars. Hardy's interest in that period stemmed from his grandparents, but he also talked to many other old people in Dorset who could remember those stirring times, including veterans of the Battle of

Above. The heath behind the cottage at Bockhampton, a tiny water-colour painted by Hardy in August 1871 when he was living at home in the cottage having just finished writing *Under the Greenwood Tree*. Dorchester can just be seen in the background. Hardy's caption on the drawing reads 'The Playground of Thomas Hardy's childhood'. He loved this unyielding landscape, populated only by furzecutters and small heathcropping ponies, and it is almost the central character in his novel *The Return of the Native*.

Waterloo, and he later visited the site of the battle. He used the contemporary local Dorset paper and worked in the British Museum for both *The Trumpet Major* and *The Dynasts*, and it always remained his favourite historical period, the only one he did serious research on.

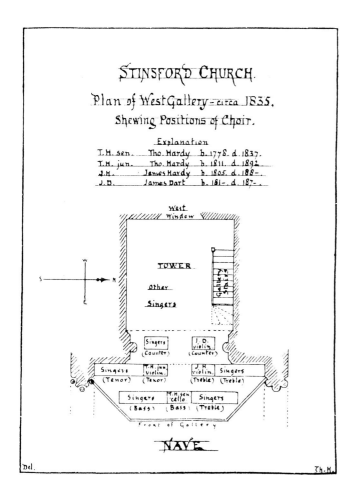

STINSFORD CHURCH.

Plan of West Gallery - circa 1835.
Shewing Positions of Choir.

Explanation
T.H. sen. — Tho. Hardy b.1778. d.1837.
T.H. jun. — Tho. Hardy b.1811. d.1892.
J.H. — James Hardy b.1805. d.188-.
J.D. — James Dart b.181-. d.187-.

West Window

TOWER
Other
Singers

Singers (Counter) — J.D. violin (Counter)

Singers (Tenor) — T.H. jun Violin (Tenor) — J.H. violin (Treble) — Singers (Treble)

Singers (Bass) — T.H. sen cello (Bass) — Singers (Treble)

Front of Gallery

NAVE

Del. — Th. H.

As a boy Hardy, helped by his father, drew this plan of where the choir sat in his grandfather's time in the gallery of Stinsford church. His grandfather (TH sen) and his cello were at the front, with Thomas Hardy junior, and his brother James Hardy and James Dart behind on violins. Most Dorset churches then had bands, but Stinsford was regarded as a particularly good one, although lacking the wind instruments found in many (eg at Puddletown). All were replaced by organs during the 19th century (Hardy catalogued the downfall of one band in his short story *A Few Crusted Characters*.)

The gallery was removed in the early 1840s so that Hardy's sketch of the Old West Gallery (*below*) must have been constructed from his father's memory of it.

Old West Gallery, Stinsford

Hardy's mother remembered the three Hardys (father and two sons) arriving at church wearing 'top hats, stick-up shirt collars, dark blue coats with great collars and gilt buttons, deep cuffs and black silk "stocks" or neckerchiefs'. Doubtless they looked smarter than Michael Mail in this illustration from the 1878 edition of Hardy's *Under the Greenwood Tree*, which centred around the Stinsford church band, and which Hardy later thought he had rather burlesqued.

The church at Stinsford, the village of which Bockhampton was a part, where Hardy's namesake grandfather, a noted bass viol (early cello) player, revitalised the church choir and band from 1801. As well as church services, the choir and band carolled round the whole parish on Christmas Eve, often not finishing until six on Christmas morning, as in the novel *Under the Greenwood Tree*. Hardy's father gave up the band in 1841 or 1842, when the novelist was only a small child. This drawing by Hardy was used as the frontispiece for his first volume of poetry in 1898.

Early Childhood

1840–1848

Hardy's mother Jemima Hand came from Melbury Osmund in North Dorset, and worked there as a cook for the Fox-Strangways. She moved to Stinsford in 1836 to be cook to the vicar. In 'A Church Romance' Hardy reconstructed her meeting with his father:

> 'She turned in the high pew, until her sight
> Swept the west gallery, and caught its row
> Of music-men with viol, book, and bow
> Against the sinking, sad tower-window light.
>
> She turned again, and in her pride's despite
> One strenuous viol's inspirer seemed to throw
> A message from his string to her below,
> Which said: 'I claim thee as my own forthright!'

They married in December 1839, when Jemima was four months pregnant. Pregnancy before marriage was common among the ordinary people of Dorset: in some places, like Portland, it was universal and the couple had to demonstrate their fertility before marriage. Thomas Hardy the third was born on 2 June 1840, at eight o'clock in the morning. He was a weak child, unlike his sturdy parents, and before he went to school neighbours thought 'that Tommy would have to be a parson, being obviously no good for any practical pursuit'.

Melancholy and pessimism were later seen as leading characteristics of Hardy, but he vehemently denied them. An early indication of pessimism was an event he distinctly remembered. As a young child (apparently only five years old) 'He was lying on his back in the sun, thinking how useless he was, and covered his face with his straw hat. The sun's rays streamed through the interstices of the straw, the lining having disappeared. Reflecting on his experiences of the world so far as he had got, he came to the conclusion that he did not want to grow up . . . he did not want at all to be a man, or to possess things, but to remain as he was, in the same spot, and to know no more people than he already knew (about half a dozen)'. Odd thoughts for such a young child, perhaps showing his mother's influence. His father was a cheerful person, handsome and something of a ladies man. His mother was far more complex, intelligent but hampered by an impoverished childhood with a drunken father.

After he was famous Hardy was outraged at being called a peasant, and always insisted his antecedents were yeomen. In *The Dorsetshire Labourer* Hardy defined the class above the labourers: 'Villages used to contain, in addition to the agricultural inhabitants, an interesting and better-informed class, ranking distinctly above those – the blacksmith, the carpenter, the shoe-maker, the small higgler [a carrier who also dealt], the shopkeeper' and he might have added the builder or mason, which is what his father was.

It is important to define the level of society Hardy was born into, not just because it affected his childhood, but because most of his fictional heroes and heroines are from the same level. Hardy exploited the potential of this class in the 19th century to rise or fall, both in fiction and in his life.

Hardy's favourite sibling, Mary was born in 1841. After her death in 1915 he wrote in a letter: 'in childhood she was almost my only companion – the others being younger – and she had always been the one with the keenest literary tastes and instincts'.

Henry was born when Thomas was ten, Kate when he was sixteen, completing the rather spread-out family. Hardy did not go to school until he was eight, being thought too frail, and unlikely to survive. In 1848 he went to the village school at Stinsford, which was well run because it was the 'hobby' of the lady of the manor, Mrs Julia Martin who lived at Kingston Maurwood house. She and her husband owned the land the Bockhampton cottage stood on, and employed the Hardy building firm a good deal. She was 'passionately fond of Tommy almost from his infancy – he is said to have been an attractive little fellow at this time – whom she had been accustomed to take into her lap and kiss until he was quite a big boy'. As this passage from the *Life* shows Hardy didn't forget her, but when he was moved to a school in Dorchester (and worse, a Non-Conformist school) Mrs Martin was furious and ceased employing the Hardy building firm.

Caption overleaf

Previous page. Puddletown was the nearest village of any size to Bockhampton, and many of Hardy's relatives lived there. He used Puddletown as Weatherbury in *Far from the Madding Crowd*. In 1851 there were 1,300 inhabitants, making it virtually a small town. This photograph was taken about 1900, but the village would have looked little different in the 1840s when he first knew it, although of course bicycles did not exist then.

Right. Jemima Hardy with her first-born, the novelist in 1841, from a painting. She was ambitious for him, her first child, and gave all her children a strong sense of family. She hoped that none of her four children would ever marry (only the novelist did) and that they would live together when grown up, which the other three did.

Below. Hardy's sister Kate in about 1866 when she was ten, and his brother Henry aged sixteen taken at about the same time. There seem to be no surviving photographs of Mary, his favourite sister. She and Kate became teachers, and Henry took over the family building business.

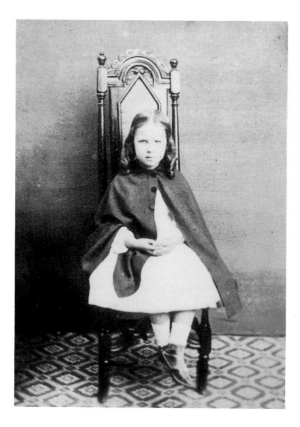

The stairs to the gallery of Puddletown church, which still survive and where Hardy's grandfather occasionally played in the church band. This faked photograph was taken in 1901 with an artist's model in mid-19th century clothes. The photographer was probably trying to illustrate *Far from the Madding Crowd*, but succeeded in producing a scene Hardy himself could have known when young.

Below and below right. Hardy's violin, still preserved in the Dorset County Museum, and a detail from one of his grandfather's music books also used by Hardy's father. Hardy bought the violin in London in the early 1860s, when he was a young man, and it was kept in his study all his life. As a child Hardy was 'extraordinarily sensitive to music' and three or four of the tunes his father played in the evenings moved him to tears. This passionate love of music lasted all his life.

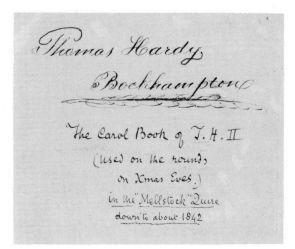

Thomas Hardy
Bockhampton

The Carol Book of T. H. II
(used on the rounds
on Xmas Eves)
in the "Mellstock" Quire
down to about 1842

Left and above. Britain's second 'talkie' was a film version of *Under the Greenwood Tree*, 1928, certainly starring the tree, but burlesquing rural Dorset severely. Margeurite Allan played Fancy Day, and John Batten as Dick Dewy. Despite the Hollywood feel, it was made in England by British International Pictures. Hardy drew on his father's memories for the band, since they ceased playing in church when he was only a year old. Hardy himself, with his father, played for many secular parties, and at Christmas.

The drawing from Hardy's notebook (*right*) shows a more realistic band.

Above. Kingston Maurwood House, the mansion of the estate which owned the cottage Hardy was born in. Mrs Martin, who lived in the big house, was the first member of the upper classes Hardy met. The contrast between this house and its grounds, and the Bockhampton cottage is severe.

Right. The grounds of Kingston Maurwood House today with the 18th century 'Grecian Temple' mentioned in Hardy's novel *Desperate Remedies*, which is set in and around the house. A neat measured plan of this 'temple or summer house' is in Hardy's architectural notebooks of the 1860s.

Thomas Hardy senior in 1877, when he was 66, and his wife Jemima taken a year earlier when she was 63. Hardy described his mother's face as showing 'dignity and judgement', although 'the Roman nose and countenance would better have suited a taller build'. She, like the novelist, felt that fate was against her. In 1870 Hardy wrote in his private notebook, 'Mother's notion, and also mine: that a figure stands in our van with arm uplifted, to knock us back from any pleasant prospect we indulge in as probable'.

Hardy's mother came from Melbury Osmund in north Dorset, the area he used for the setting of *The Woodlanders*. This modern view of an adjacent village, Melbury Bubb, is taken from the chalk down which bounds the extensive vale. Hardy particularly admired views from the down: 'every hedge studded with trees'.

The mummers in the Hardy Players' *Return of the Native* with the heroine Eustacia, who joined them anonymously, on the extreme left. This Christmas play was called the play of St George locally, and Hardy saw it performed in the traditional manner in his childhood. On Christmas night 1920 the Hardy players came to Max Gate, Hardy's home, and performed the play for him.

Right. A Hardy heroine come to life: Gertrude Bugler as Eustacia Vye in *The Return of the Native*, dramatised by the Hardy Players in 1920. The novel is set in the heathland to the east of Hardy's birthplace in the 1840s, the time of Hardy's childhood, and incorporates many of his memories. Hardy was captivated by Gertrude Bugler's impersonations of his heroines.

Dorchester, School and Architecture

1850–1862

By sending Hardy to a 'superior' school in Dorchester when he was ten, his mother started the process which would remove him from the class he was born into and elevate him into the professions. Going to school was not even compulsory when Hardy was young, and those who did go usually left at twelve. Hardy was an avid reader from a young age, and a good student. Many of the upper classes thought that the children of the lower classes should not be educated, or they would leave their lowly jobs. Hardy and his mother had to sit through a sermon at Stinsford in 1856 in which the vicar preached against the presumption shown by one of the lower class trying to rise by becoming an architect, just after Hardy had become a pupil architect.

In 1853 the headmaster set up a new school, for older and more advanced pupils, and Hardy went with him, learning latin as an extra. Clearly from this time he was not intended by his mother to take over the family building business. Henry's birth in 1851

Left. Thomas Hardy aged sixteen, about the time he started work for Hicks the architect in Dorchester. At this time he joined the crowd of three or four thousand which assembled to see Martha Browne hung at Dorchester Prison for the murder of her husband. Seventy years later in a letter he remembered 'what a fine figure she showed against the sky as she hung in the misty rain, and how the tight black silk gown set off her shape as she wheeled half round and back'.

may have helped form this decision: he did take over the business. When he was sixteen Hardy went to work for Hicks, a Dorchester architect, his parents paying for his three years pupilage. Hardy 'cheerfully agreed' to this, but at that time he wished to become a clergyman. He continued working on his Latin while with Hicks and took up Greek, keeping up the genteel part of his education. His working on the classics every morning from six to eight (or even from four am in the summer) may have been less regular than he later claimed, but he certainly lived an unusual life during his five years with Hicks. He worked 'in a county town of assizes and aldermen, which had advanced to railways and telegraphs and daily London papers; yet not living there, but walking in every day from a world of shepherds and ploughmen' making with his study of the classics 'a triple existence unusual for a young man . . . a life twisted of three strands – the professional life, the scholar's life, and the rustic life'. Part of the rustic life was playing the violin, sometimes alone, sometimes with his father and uncle, for weddings, christenings or Christmas parties.

Going to school in Dorchester expanded the number of people Hardy knew, a normal part of growing up, and while at school his life-long series of infatuations with girls or women started. He himself records several which recur fifty or even sixty years later in his poetry, including Louisa who was sent to a school in Weymouth. Hardy managed to find out which church the school attended, by going to Weymouth Sunday after Sunday, but got no further than shy smiles. Normal adolescent behaviour, but with Hardy these infatuations continued all his life.

Working for Hicks he met yet more people, and travelled within the county to make drawings of buildings (particularly churches as Hicks specialised in church rebuilding), and started to get to know more of the county he would later describe so well. At this time Hardy was a regular church-goer, and a very 'churchy' young man. He started writing poetry about the time he began work, and also produced some short prose, none of which was published and little of which survives. He knew William Barnes, the Dorset poet, because his school was next door to Hick's office, and Hardy would run round there and ask him to solve grammatical disputes in the office.

Like his childhood, Hardy's twelve years in school and at work in Dorchester were very important, with themes and settings from this time occurring all through his fiction, and personal recollections fifty or sixty years old surfacing in his poetry.

Dorchester, the county town of Dorset, where Hardy went to school and where he worked until he was twenty-one. The photographs date from 1860 when he was working at Hick's office in South Street, one of the buildings just seen on the left of the photograph (*left*). On the right is the town grammar school founded by another Thomas Hardy in Elizabethan times. South Walks (*above*) runs from the end of the street Hardy worked in, close to the office, and is one of several tree-lined promenades laid out on the line of the Roman town walls which encircled the town. The

centre of Dorchester includes St Peter's Church (*above*), where Hardy helped with a restoration in 1856. His novel *The Mayor of Casterbridge* vividly describes Dorchester as Casterbridge in the 1850s, the time he knew as a boy and young man. In his speech accepting the freedom of the borough of Dorchester in 1910 Hardy said that 'freedom of the Borough of Dorchester did seem something that I had possessed a long while, had helped myself to.'

Thomas Hardy, a very young-looking nineteen, the student architect, taken in a formal photographers' setting, typical of the time. In 'The Passer-By' written in his eighties Hardy describes himself at this time, as he imagines Louisa saw him

'He used to pass, well-trimmed and brushed,
    My window every day,
And when I smiled on him he blushed,
That youth, quite as girl might; aye,
    In the shyest way'

William Barnes aged about fifty. When the sixteen-year-old Hardy started work in the house next to Barnes's in Dorchester, the poet was fifty five and had already published two volumes of his poetry in the Dorset dialect. Two more volumes came out while Hardy was his neighbour, including his best known poem 'Linden Lea': 'Ithin the woodlands, flow'ry gleaded,/By the woak tree's mossy moot,/ The sheenen grassbleades timber-sheaded,/Now do quiver under voot'. Barnes revived the name of 'Wessex', later taken on by Hardy for the area where his novels were set.

The eighty-six year old Hardy surrounded by characters from *The Mayor of Casterbridge*, before a performance by the Barnes Theatre Company in Weymouth in 1926. A strange photograph, the aged author with representations of characters he invented to set in the background of the town he knew so well as a boy and young man. The theatrical costumes matched those he then saw daily. At Weymouth he was greeted by great ovations inside and outside the theatre.

Top right. Charminster church undergoing restoration in 1895. Hardy, who worked on church restoration from 1856 to 1872, described and regretted the church restoration mania of the middle and later 19th century in a speech to the Society for the Protection of Ancient Buildings in 1906, looking 'back in a contrite spirit at my own brief experience as a church-restorer, and recalling instances of the drastic treatment we then dealt out with light hearts to the unlucky fanes that fell into our hands'. From the 1880s he helped SPAB in trying to control the repair of medieval buildings, retraining architects to truly repair rather than rebuild.

Right. Fordington High Street about 1895. The Vicarage where the Moule family lived was at the top of this small hill. The picturesque thatched cottages conceal the fact that even by the 1890s Fordington was horribly overcrowded, with a population density as high as that of Manchester.

The Mill Street Mission, Fordington in about 1910.
Fifty years earlier, when Hardy knew this large
village (a suburb of Dorchester), it was even more
crowded and unhealthy. In 1854 cholera broke
out, and was only contained by the Rev Henry
Moule, who fearlessly nursed his parishioners.
Hardy recalled this heroism in a short story 'A
Changed Man,' and described Fordington (called
Durnover) in *The Mayor of Casterbridge*.

Horace Moule, a close friend of Hardy and a
published poet by the time they met in about 1856.
He was eight years older than Hardy, and had
been to Oxford and Cambridge although he
received no degree from either. He helped Hardy
with his Greek, and guided his reading into liberal
channels. Handsome and brilliantly clever, Moule
was a depressive and an alcoholic. At the end of
his life Hardy described Moule as the 'confidant
and guide' of his youth and early manhood, and
Moule occurs as 'my friend' in Hardy's poetry
right to the end of Hardy's life.

The Moule family outside their home, Fordington vicarage, in 1869. Hardy knew the whole family, calling the sons 'the seven brethren' (the eighth in the photograph must be a sister's husband). The oldest, Henry (third from left) corrected Hardy's attempts at water colour in the late '50s, and Horace (fifth from the right) was his particular friend. The parents, the Rev Henry Moule and his wife, are seated centre. Doubtless the bookish Hardy would have preferred to have been born into an academic family like this one: two of the brothers became bishops, and two more clergymen.

London, Cornwall and First Fiction

1862–1873

In April 1862, when he was nearly 22, Hardy left Dorset for London, to 'pursue the art and science of architecture on more advanced lines'. It is possible that disappointment at a proposal of marriage being refused speeded him on his way, but if he intended to pursue a career in architecture, it was a good move. He carefully bought a return ticket, which he preserved for six months as an escape route if he couldn't get employment.

In fact he got a job within a month, with Arthur Blomfield a well-known architect, and stayed with him for five years working as an assistant architect and living in lodgings in Kilburn. In 1865 an article by Hardy – a skit called 'How I built myself a house' written to amuse the pupils in the office – was published in *Chambers's Journal*. He was paid £3.15s, his first literary earnings. Until 1866 he still hoped to become a clergyman, and that year also saw a great outpouring of poetry, which may be related to his later statement that he was a child until he was sixteen, and a youth until he was twenty-five. Certainly he was involved with young women while he was in London, and may have been engaged. From 1866 he sent poetry to several magazines, but it was all rejected.

Hardy went to plays, concerts and operas, and constantly visited picture galleries and exhibitions, and even appeared at Covent Garden as an extra. He still read widely especially poetry, studied the classics, and saw Henry Moule when he visited London. He returned home (or to his sister Mary when she was away teaching) for Christmas and holidays so there was no rift with his family.

After five years in London, Hardy's health was suffering, and when his old employer Hicks wrote to ask if he knew of a good assistant, Hardy returned to Dorchester and his health immediately improved. This return must have been seen as a failure by Hardy himself and his family, but he immediately started writing his first novel *The Poor Man and the Lady*, and in July 1868 submitted it to Macmillans, the publishers. Alexander Macmillan 'read the novel with much interest and admiration' but thought Hardy's upper class characters were unrealistic. His reader described it as 'like some clever lad's dream', but he and the publisher advised Hardy to go on writing, but to improve his plots. Hardy made alterations to the manuscript, and resubmitted it to Macmillan and other publishers, but with no success.

Hicks died, but Hardy was taken on by Crickmay, a Weymouth architect who had bought the business, and from May 1869 he worked and lived in Weymouth for nine months. Taking the advice of the publishers very seriously he started his sensational novel *Desperate Remedies*, a romantic mystery reusing parts of *The Poor Man and the Lady*. This new novel was declined by Macmillans in March 1870, but the second publisher, Tinsley, accepted it if Hardy would pay £75 towards the cost of publishing, halving the profits (if any) with the publisher. Hardy agreed, and it was published anonymously in March 1871.

After *Desperate Remedies* was amost complete, but before it was accepted for publication, Hardy went to St Juliot on the north Cornwall coast, to examine a church which Crickmay was to rebuild. Leaving Bockhampton at four in the morning, he arrived at St. Juliot in the dark of early evening, and Emma Gifford the vicar's sister-in-law was there to greet him. As she later wrote 'scarcely any author and his wife could have had a much more romantic meeting'. They fell immediately in love, and Hardy stayed longer for his first visit than intended, and returned as often as he could. Each found the other glamorous, reflecting the romantic (if stern) landscape, but probably Hardy was less sophisticated than she thought him; and Emma was not so securely middle class as Hardy thought and probably pretended to be five years younger than she was.

The first review of *Desperate Remedies* was good, but the second bad and Hardy remembered the second one all his life. Within three months the book was remaindered, selling for 2/6 for the three volumes.

For the next two years Hardy worked intermittently in London for a couple of different architects, and wrote *Under the Greenwood Tree*, responding to suggestions that rustic characters and scenery were what he did best. He submitted it to Macmillans late in 1871, and they refused it with their reader suggesting that the author 'would do well to shut his ears to the fooleries of critics', something Hardy was never able to do. Emma encouraged him to persist in his writing, and a chance meeting with Tinsley his earlier publisher led to Hardy selling him the copyright of *Under the Greenwood Tree*, which was published in May 1872 to good reviews. Tinsley asked Hardy for a novel which would run as a serial in his magazine, a common method of publishing novels then. Hardy offered him *A Pair of Blue Eyes*, which he had already started, but abandoned. For the last six months of 1872 he lived at Bockhampton steadily writing the novel which was serialised as he wrote it, and published in book form in May 1873.

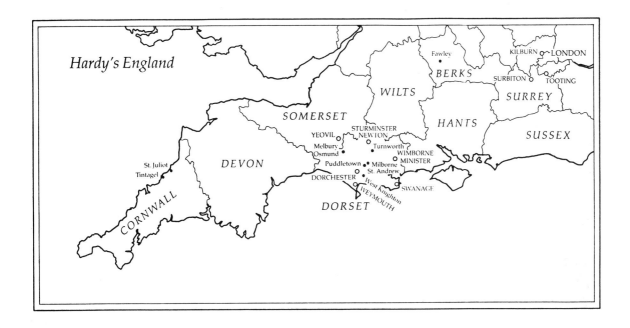

Hardy aged 21, at about the time he went to work in London, a copy given to the second Mrs Hardy more than forty years later. He described himself as 'quite a pink-faced youth' even then. For two years before he went to London he was paid 15s (75p) a week by Hicks, and lived in lodgings in Dorchester during the week, returning home to Bockhampton for weekends.

Adelphi Terrace, designed by the Adam brothers and built right on the Thames in the 1770s. Hardy worked in offices on the first floor for five years, being paid £110 a year as an assistant architect. He enjoyed the cheerful irreverence of the people he worked with: they all got into trouble for dangling rude notes on bits of string over the heads of members of the Reform League who had the offices below. Hardy retained an affection for the building, asking a friend to photograph it in 1906. This may be one of the photographs taken for him then. Adelphi Terrace was demolished in 1937.

The view from Adelphi Terrace, taken in 1902.
When Hardy was working there in the 1860s
Victoria embankment was being built, putting the
gardens seen here between the building and the
river. He later claimed to have seen the first barge-
load of soil for the Embankment thrown into the
water. Waterloo Bridge (left) is the one he would
have known, finished in 1817 but now replaced.

Hardy described the office as 'capital', telling his
sister Mary that they could see from their
windows 'right across the Thames, and on a clear
day every bridge is visible'. Waterloo station,
where he caught trains to come home to Dorset is
on the right in the background behind the shot
tower.

The Thames slightly down river from Hardy's office, with St. Pauls and part of the city of London, in the 1860s when Hardy was working there. The contrast between sleepy Dorchester and the bustle and sheer size of London must have been dramatic: London's population was 3 million, nearly 500 times Dorchester's. London was the richest city in the world, but with many poor. Hardy explored the capital thoroughly, later being glad that he had seen it before it was modernised and stopped being the city described by Dickens and Thackeray. The shores of the Thames before the Embankments were built consisted of wharfs and warehouses set in the river mud. Hardy blamed the stench from the sewage-decorated mud at low tide for the ill-health which drove him back to Dorset after five years working in London.

London Bridge in the 1860s, the time Hardy was working there.

Henry Mayhew described the life of London's poor in 1861, including the street sellers, beggars and prostitutes who worked the streets. In Regent Street and the Haymarket 'the brilliant illumination of the shops, cafes, Turkish divans, assembly halls, and concert rooms' strikes the visitor, as does 'the troops of elegantly dressed courtesans, rustling in silks and satins, promenading along these superb streets among throngs of fashionable people, and persons of apparently every order and pursuit, from the ragged crossing-sweeper and tattered shoe-black to the high-bred gentleman of fashion'.

The house where Hardy lodged for four years from 1863, 16 Westbourne Park Gardens, Bayswater, just west of Paddington station and very close to the middle of London. Hardy's London lodging were all in middle-class areas: he avoided the capital's extremes. Here Hardy studied poetry, making lists of words and phrases, notes for poems, and reading extensively. He thought that reading for six hours every evening contributed to the ill-health which made him leave London.

Hardy in proper London clothes, including a top hat and umbrella, taken after he had been in London for a year. In the same year, 1863, he won two small prizes from the Architectural Association for an essay on 'On the Application of coloured bricks and Terra Cotta to Modern Architecture' and for a design for a country mansion.

A sketch made by Hardy from St James Park in April 1863, with the Houses of Parliament in the background (Big Ben left and Victoria Tower right) framing Westminster Abbey. Among his many expeditions in London Hardy heard Lord Palmerston, the veteran parliamentarian who had been War Secretary during the Napoleonic wars (always a time which fascinated Hardy) speak in the House of Commons, and also managed to attend Palmerston's funeral in Westminster Abbey in 1865, getting a ticket for a high seat with a good view. Hardy was delighted to get into the funeral of a man whose life overlapped those of Pitt, Fox, Sheridan, Burke etc. many of whom occur in his epic verse drama *The Dynasts* written forty years later. In 1863 Hardy would presumably have been startled had he known that his own ashes were to be buried in Westminster Abbey.

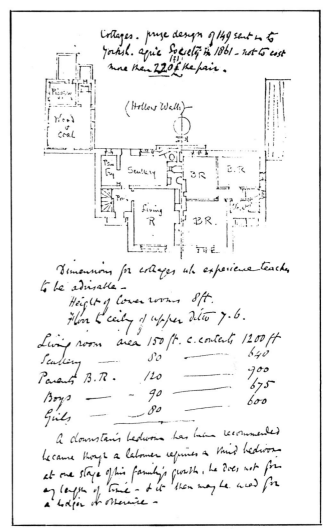

Above and left. Although Hardy did not particularly enjoy architecture, he must have worked reasonably hard and been a satisfactory employee as he could always get a job. He kept an architectural notebook with notes and drawings on a wide range of architecture from the 1862-72, including decorative ironwork, and a copy of a plan for labourers' cottages.

A drawing for the 'restoration' of Turnworth church in central Dorset, designed by Hardy in 1869 when he was working for Crickmay. This is the only church Hardy designed on his own. The tower of the medieval church was allowed to survive, but a completely new nave with compex carved stone capitals was substituted for the medieval one. Forty years later Hardy recalled that full 'restoration' involved demolishing the whole church and starting from scratch, and he acknowledged that the whole restoration movement had destroyed and damaged far more churches than simple neglect would have done.

From the 1890s Hardy was friendly with the vicar of Turnworth, Thomas Perkins, and often visited the vicarage (right in lower photograph). Perkins was an unusual man, a vegetarian and passionate antivivisectionist, and a keen photographer. Hardy was also strongly against vivisection and felt keenly the sufferings of animals.

Tryphena Sparks, one of Hardy's Puddletown cousins, one of several local girls Hardy was infatuated with. He was probably involved earlier with her two elder sisters, since there is a family tradition that Hardy had wanted to marry each of the three sisters, and had given Phena an engagement ring. She went to train as a teacher just before Hardy met Emma. In 1890 he started to write a poem about her, not knowing that she was dying. 'Thoughts of Phena' calls her his 'lost prize'.

Weymouth Bay, about 1878, with the harbour
entrance left and the start of the bay right. Hardy
lived here for most of 1869, when it was still a
fashionable resort, if not so important as it had
been in the years around 1800 when George III
and his court spent the summers there. Hardy
swam in the sea before work in the morning, and
rowed in the bay in the evening, just as the hero of
the book he was writing did. *Desperate Remedies*
also includes a trip by paddleboat, like the one
seen here. Weymouth, called Budmouth, features
in several of Hardy's novels, in *The Trumpet Major*
its hey-day with George III is recreated.

Hardy aged about twenty-nine, still looking
young despite the newly-grown beard. This
photograph was taken in Weymouth while Hardy
was working there as an architect and writing
Desperate Remedies, despite being distracted by the
lively town. He joined a dancing-class, and was
not dismayed to find it 'a gay gathering for dances
and love-making by adepts of both sexes'. In order
to finish the novel he left Weymouth and went
home to Bockhampton.

Bench Ends - St. Juliot Church - Cornwall
1870

J. Hardy. del.

Bench-ends at St Juliot church, Cornwall, drawn
by Hardy in 1870. He sent his drawings with the
photograph of the church before its restoration, to
the vicar of St Juliot after Emma's death in 1913, as
a memorial of their meeting there and a reminder
of what the church was like before it was
'restored'. St Juliot church was in a bad way before
the restoration, Emma recalling that these bench
ends were rotting and 'the ivy hung gaily from the
roof timbers'. The tower and north transept were
demolished, and all the old woodwork (including
the bench ends) destroyed. Hardy instructed the
builder to repair the old chancel screen, but the
builder decided in Hardy's absence that he
wouldn't 'stand on a pound or two' while he was
about it, and made a new screen 'instead of that
patched-up old thing', the ancient oak going to
boil up the workmen's tea-kettles.

Left. The Rectory, St Juliot, where Emma lived with her sister and brother-in-law. Her sister was thirty-five years younger than her husband, and Emma had lived with them since their marriage three years before, probably to escape having to take a job as a governess or companion. The sisters' father, a solicitor, was a difficult man who was often drunk, Emma was middle class, but poor. Hardy's mother called her 'poor gentry'.

Lower left. An early photograph of the view from the Rectory, St Juliot, where Emma lived. After his first professional visit, Hardy returned as often as he could to visit Emma, who copied out his manuscripts for him and encouraged him greatly in his writing. Emma and the wild landscape of north Cornwall are mixed together in many of Hardy's poems.

Below. Thomas Hardy and Emma Gifford as they were at the time of their four year courtship. Both were the same age. Hardy at 32 looks mature with the beard he grew (perhaps as a literary gesture) after he started writing. Emma's 'corn-coloured hair, abundant in its coils', was much admired by Hardy, who found her 'so living', full of the physical vitality he lacked.

Imaginary View of Tintagel Castle.
at the time of the tragedy.   T. H.
                                               May 1923.

Tintagel Castle, perhaps the most magical spot on
the north Cornwall coast. Emma and Hardy
visited it in 1870, during their courtship, and were
locked in because they lingered too long, 'only
narrowly escaping being imprisoned there for the
night by much signalling with handkerchiefs to
cottagers in the valley'. In 1916 he revisited
Tintagel with his second wife, and as a result
wrote seven years later *The Famous Tragedy of the
Queen of Cornwall*, a short play in verse 'a new
version of an old story': the love of Tristram and
Iseult set in Tintagel Castle.

Above. As a frontispiece for the play Hardy drew
a reconstruction of the castle, his last drawing
produced at the age of 83.

Beeny Cliff, near St Juliot, the setting of one of the heroes' falls in *A Pair of Blue Eyes*, and often visited by Emma and Hardy during their courtship. The pencil drawing by him dated August 1870 is annotated by Emma 'It never looks like summer', and Hardy used this as the title of a poem in 1913, written on a pilgrimage to Cornwall after Emma's death:

> "It never looks like summer here
>   On Beeny by the sea."
> But though she saw its look as drear,
>   Summer it seemed to me.
>
> It never looks like summer now
>   Whatever weather's there;
> But ah, it cannot anyhow,
>   On Beeny or elsewhere!

> BOSCASTLE
> March 8, 1913

DESPERATE REMEDIES.

A Novel.

"Though a course of adventures which are only connected with each other by having happened to the same individual is what most frequently occurs in nature, yet the province of the romance-writer being artificial, there is more required from him than a mere compliance with the simplicity of reality."

Sir W. Scott.

IN THREE VOLUMES.

VOL. I.

LONDON:
TINSLEY BROTHERS, 18, CATHERINE ST., STRAND.
1871.

[The Right of Translation is Reserved.]

Hardy, in common with all authors, never forgot 'the thrill that ran through me from head to foot when I held my first copy of *Desperate Remedies* in my hand'. This, his first book, was anonymous, although rather grandly translation rights were reserved. Sadly for Hardy he could also never forget any parts of a review which were bad and the *Spectator's* review referring to the novel as 'a desperate remedy for an emaciated purse' along with the suggestion that the author wasn't brave enough to reveal his name, made him wish he was dead when he read it sitting on a stile at Kingston Maurwood. When he was rich enough he employed a cuttings agency to send him reviews, a foolish thing for one so sensitive.

Success and Marriage

1873–1883

From the middle of 1872, when he was thirty-two, Hardy was a full-time writer, no longer having to use architecture as a support. During the next ten rather unsettled years, he wrote seven novels, half his total output. Leslie Stephen, editor of the prestigious *Cornhill* Magazine, wrote to Hardy about a serial in the autumn of 1872 because he was impressed with *Under the Greenwood Tree*. Tinsley was paying £200 for the serial Hardy was then writing, but Stephen offered £400 for what was to become *Far from the Madding Crowd*, almost four times what Hardy had been earning a year as an assistant architect.

Hardy told Stephen that he lived with his family at Bockhampton to write the novel, because 'it is within a walk of the district in which the incidents are supposed to occur. I find it a great advantage to be actually among the poeple described at the time of describing them'. In September 1873, just after he had started the novel, Horace Moule committed suicide in Cambridge. Hardy was devastated, but managed to produce his chapters on time. Moule went on appearing in Hardy's poetry right to the end of Hardy's life, fifty-five years later. He completed the novel, sometimes having to gallop to keep ahead of the printers, in July 1874, and in September he and Emma Gifford were married in London, four years after they had first met. None of Hardy's family was present, and only Emma's uncle a clergyman, who married them, and one of her brothers.

The honeymoon trip to Rouen and Paris was Hardy's first visit abroad. On their return they rented a house in Surbiton, a remote London suburb, but in March 1875 they moved rather closer to London. By this time Hardy was writing *The Hand of Ethelberta*, a rather melodramatic romp, apparently produced to demonstrate that he could write urban novels in contrast to *Far from the Madding Crowd*. For ten months from July 1875 they lived in lodgings at Swanage, then a small seaside village, where part of the novel was set. It was published as a serial in *Cornhill*, and in an American magazine, and although quite well received, did not have the success of *Far from the Madding Crowd*.

In 1876, in another magazine, the first of his poetry was published. After the novel was finished the Hardys moved to Yeovil and then in May went to Holland and the Rhine, visiting the site of the battle of Waterloo on the way back. On her return Emma complained that they had 'no home and no chosen county', but soon after they moved for the first time into an unfurnished house at Sturminster Newton in the middle of Dorset. Here Hardy wrote *The Return of the Native*, now considered one of his finest books but refused by Stephen for *Cornhill*. Hardy had difficulty selling it, and got only half the price he received for the *Hand of Ethelberta* as a serial.

The Hardys were in their middle 30s when they moved to Sturminster Newton, and had been married only two years. While they were there they clearly hoped for children, but in vain. However, Hardy later described their two years sojourn there as 'our happiest time'.

In March 1878 they moved to Tooting, because Hardy thought the proximity of London would be better professionally. He joined clubs, both went to concerts, the theatre and picture galleries, and were generally more sociable than when in Dorset. Much research in the British Museum Reading Room for *The Tumpet Major* was needed to supplement his grandparent's memories, and he was working on this book through to the end of 1879. Leslie Stephen complained that the heroine of *The Trumpet Major* married the wrong man. Hardy replied that they usually did, but Stephen retorted 'Not in magazines'. Hardy also produced short stories for magazine publication.

After a trip to France, Hardy started his ninth novel *A Laodicean*, which had been sold, like all his others, as a magazine serial before more than a few chapters were written.

Hardy fell seriously ill, probably with kidney stones. He was given the classic Victorian, medically useless advice to stay in bed for months (nearly six!) and had to dictate most of the novel to Emma. Now convinced that London was bad for his health, and his writing, the Hardys seem to have decided to make Dorset their permanent home, and moved to a rented house in Wimborne as soon as he was well.

Here they stayed for two years, joining in some of the town's social life, such as Shakespeare readings, and attending a ball at Canford House, but also visiting Scotland and Paris and returning to London for part of the season. Hardy wrote *Two on a Tower*, partly set near Wimborne, and several short stories. He later admitted that he should have rewritten the novel for volume publication, but 'played truant' and went off to Paris instead.

Hardy aged about forty, when he was writing his eighth novel *A Laodicean*. After he stopped writing novels he was dismissive about his fiction. Typically when writing to his friend Gosse in 1918 he said 'For the relief of my necessities, as the Prayer Book puts it, I began writing novels and made a sort of trade of it'. This does not reflect his attitude when he was actually working on them:

Hardy told Stephen who asked for some alterations in Hardy's first really successful book *Far from the Madding Crowd* that 'present circumstances lead me to wish to be considered a good hand at a serial' while 'I may have higher aims some day, and be a great stickler for the proper artistic balance of the completed work'.

Left.   One of Helen Paterson's illustrations for the magazine serial and the first edition of *Far from the Madding Crowd*. Hardy supplied her with sketches of rural scenes and objects, and although they only met a few times, it is clear from a later poem that she was one of the many young women Hardy was infatuated with. Both she and Hardy married other people in the same year, Hardy's marriage with Emma being made possible by the success of the novel. Under her married name Helen Allingham, she became well known for pretty country watercolours.

Lower left.   The harvest supper scene from the 1967 film of *Far From the Madding Crowd*, directed by John Schlesinger (standing on the extreme right), A Joseph Janni – Vic Films Production from Anglo Amalgamated. Julie Christie as Bathsheba Everdene (seated in the window), Alan Bates as Gabriel Oak, Peter Finch as William Boldwood and Terence Stamp as Sergeant Troy. The farmworkers now wear suits, not smocks.

Below.   Swanage in the 1880s, still partly a fishing and quarrying village, and partly a seaside resort, as it had been when the Hardys lived there for nine months in 1875-76. They lodged with a sea-captain very like the one described in *The Hand of Ethelberta* which Hardy was writing while they were there. The novel is partly set in Swanage.

Sturminster Newton, three photographs taken by William Barnes' son in 1883, only five years after Hardy lived there. The small town was even more remote than Dorchester, and Hardy was conscious that William Barnes was born here and had set much of his poetry in the surrounding Blackmore Vale. Hardy and Emma rowed on the River Stour, finding the weed so thick it was difficult to move; below their house the river looks just like the part photographed above. Robert Young, another dialect poet, told them that his grandfather, with the rest of the population, was so excited when the mail coach first ran through, that he got up early and swept the whole street (*upper right*) and sprinkled it with sand. Hardy always collected such stories of the local past. Sturminster Newton Mill (*right*) is downstream from the Hardy's home, just under the rivercliff rather than on it as their house is. From the back of the Hardys' house is a distant view of the Mill, from just this angle.

Riverside Villa, Sturminster Newton, taken about 1900, the Hardys' first real home. They rented the brand new semi-detached house unfurnished from 1876, and bought £100 worth of furniture for it in two hours in Bristol. The house stands on a small river cliff overlooking the River Stour, and in the upstairs front room (centre) with an extensive view over the river, Hardy wrote *The Return of the Native*. On the right is one of the two monkey puzzle trees Hardy planted in the garden.

The Hardy Players in their costumes for the play *Far from the Madding Crowd* outside the house where Hardy wrote *The Return of the Native*. They visited in June 1921, after performing part of the play in the castle ruins at Sturminster Newton. Hardy and the cast had tea at Riverside Villa.

An illustration from the serialisation of *The Return of the Native* written while the Hardys were living in Sturminster Newton, but set on the heath close to his birthplace. Hardy particularly admired this drawing, writing to the illustrator, Arthur Hopkins, to tell him that he had precisely caught Eustacia's rebelliousness.

Left. 172 Trinity Road, Tooting, where the Hardys lived for three years from 1878. *The Trumpet Major* and *A Laodicean* were written here, and Hardy was elected to the Savile Club, the principal London literary club.

Right and lower right. A picturesque view of Milborne St Andrew, Dorset, about 1890, all thatched cottages and children with firewood, contrasts with the occupants of a cottage in the same village evicted in 1874 for joining Joseph Arch's Union of Agricultural Workers and going on strike for a 2s increase on their 12s a week wages. Hardy understood the hardships labourers suffered, and heard Arch speak at a meeting of Dorset labourers in the early 1870s, finding him a moderate and sensible man, not an agitator. Farmers tried to destroy the Union by evicting members from their tied houses, or locking them out from work, and by 1889 they had succeeded.

The Minster, Wimborne in 1878, after the closure of the graveyard in 1856 and its tidying up. Hardy's poem 'The levelled churchyard' written at Wimborne in 1882 deals with the confusion after the gravestones had been moved:

> "Where we are huddled none can trace,
>   And if our names remain,
> They pave some path or passing place
>   Where we have never laid!
>
> "Here's not a modest maiden elf
>   But dreads the final Trumpet,
> Lest half of her should rise herself,
>   And half some sturdy strumpet!

The Avenue, Wimborne, where the Hardys lived from June 1881 for two years, renting a house very like the one on the right, then a modern villa. The lime trees along the road were planted while the Hardys lived there. This photograph was taken in 1903, after the trees had grown up. All the houses the Hardys rented were modern, redbrick and urban.

Max Gate and Last Fiction

1883–1895

In 1883, after nine years of marriage and a variety of homes, the Hardys came to live in Dorchester. They had previously avoided the county town, not living closer than Wimborne or Sturminster Newton – both more than 20 miles away. This seems to have been because Emma did not get on with Hardy's strongminded mother: probably no wife of Hardy could have suited her. The two had met, with Emma spending Christmas 1876 and a summer holiday with his family, but they were never close.

Hardy was 43 when he returned to Dorchester, a famous novelist and earning as much money as one of the upper classes. A token of his acceptance as one of Dorset's middle classes was his appointment as a JP less than a year after his return. They now spent part of each year in London for the 'season' to visit friends, see pictures and go to concerts, and were visited by local friends like Henry Moule, curator of the Dorset County Museum, and London ones like the writer and critic Edmund Gosse. This pattern continued, with modification for increasing age, for the rest of his life. After they moved to Dorchester they travelled more, and Hardy produced novels more slowly, presumably because he was now financially more secure.

At first they rented a house (now demolished) in the middle of Dorchester, but they bought a plot just outside the town to build themselves a house.

While living in the middle of the town Hardy wrote *The Mayor of Casterbridge*, set in Dorchester in the 1850s, the time when he was at school and working there. He supplemented his memories by reading the local weekly paper *The Dorset County Chronical* from 1826 onwards, and produced a very complete picture of the town and its people. For once he was writing ahead of serialisation. The novel was finished in April 1885 and was not due to the magazine until 1886.

The Woodlanders, his next novel (written at Max Gate), a story he had had in mind for some time, is set in the middle of Dorset where his mother grew up. He was later to say that as a story, he liked this one better than any of his novels, and perhaps this was because it reflected some of his mother's memories. The editor of the magazine it was written for doubted the propriety of parts of the story (to be plain about the sex), something Hardy was to have trouble about with later novels.

During the 1880s Hardy's social life expanded from literary circles into the upper classes, especially when he was in London, but also including visits to country houses. Hardy's sense of humour is shown in all his fiction and some of the poetry, and usually he could be amused by his own problems. In 1887, writing to his friend Gosse Hardy discussed despondency 'you would be quite shocked if I were to tell you how many weeks and months in bygone years I have gone to bed wishing never to see daylight again'. It seldom recurs now. 'One day I was saying to myself "Why art thou so heavy, O my soul, & why art thou so disquieted within me?" I could not help answering "Because you eat that pastry after a long walk, & would not profit by experience". Hardy concluded that the stomach was a main cause of despondency, but not the only one.

His most famous novel, *Tess of the D'Urbervilles*, was started in 1888, but was refused by four magazines which had requested a serial from Hardy because of 'its improper explicitness'. Even the magazine in which it was finally published asked for alterations: Tess and the other dairy maids had to be propelled across the flooded lane in a wheelbarrow, not carried by the hero. They also refused to publish the chapters on Tess's seduction and the christening of Tess's child, which was printed in other magazines. Hardy restored the cuts for volume publication in 1891, and the novel was a best seller, causing controversy. Inevitably Hardy was upset by some of the reviews: 'if this sort of thing continues no more novel-writing for me. A man must be a fool to deliberately stand up to be shot at'. As well as being shot at, he was lionised.

After *Tess* and before his last novel, Hardy wrote a strange short novel *The Well-Beloved*, serialised in 1892 but not published in book form until 1897. The hero's final position, in the original version, married to an old and difficult wife, was thought by some in Dorchester to reflect the Hardy's marriage, which was certainly uncomfortable by this time. Emma had started a private diary complaining about her husband in 1891 and to many people they met in the 1890s they seemed an ill-matched pair.

In 1893-4 Hardy acted as an architect for the last time, overseeing the restoration of West Knighton church. His brother Henry was the builder, and possibly working on building again gave Hardy some of the background for his next and final novel *Jude the Obscure*. This book upset Emma severely with what she saw as an attack on marriage and Christianity. The outline of the story had been thought out a few years earlier although not started until 1893. It was serialised in 1895 under one of its five different original titles *Hearts Insurgent*, and was, like *Tess*, heavily cut to make it suitable for family reading. The full text was published late the same year, now called *Jude the Obscure*, to some very hostile reviews – 'Hardy the Degenerate', 'Jude the Obscene'. Hardy never forgot or forgave the reviews or reviewers, and although he was level-headed enough to be amused by a bishop burning the book (recalling that it was thick and hence difficult to burn) he was less happy about the same bishop having successfully asked W H Smiths to remove the book from their influential libraries. Even his good friend Gosse told him it was the most indecent novel ever written. It sold 20,000 copies in 3 months.

The Mayor of Casterbridge

by Thomas Hardy.

Author of "Far from the Madding Crowd", "A Pair of Blue Eyes", &c.

Chapter I.

One evening of late summer, before the present century had
~~hardly reached its~~ middle-age, a young man & woman, the
latter carrying a child, were approaching the large village
of Weydon=Priors on foot. They were plainly but not ill clad,
though the thick ~~covering~~ hour of dust which had accumulated on their
shoes & clothing from an obviously long journey ~~added~~ lent a disadvantageous / shabbiness

The first page of *The Mayor of Casterbridge*, which Hardy started to write in Dorchester in 1883. All Hardy's novels were written by hand, with a dip pen. He preserved the pens with which he wrote each one, incising the novel's title into the handles. Some can still be seen on his desk in the reconstructed study in the Dorset County Museum. Emma helped him by copying out parts of the early novels, and Florence introduced him to the typewriter, by typing out some of his poems and correspondence.

Looking up Dorchester High Street in about 1890. It was just about here that in 1884 Hardy was struck by how romantic four itinerant girl musicians looked in the evening, in silvery light, whereas by daylight they had looked coarse: a typically detailed observation by Hardy, who noticed everything. Hardy had explored every alley and corner of Dorchester as a child, and it was his home town for three-quarters of his life.

Left. St Peter's church in the centre of Dorchester in 1887. The building in the middle with Gothic windows is the brand new Dorset County Museum, often visited by Hardy. In the corner between the church and museum a statue of his friend Barnes was erected the following year. Although Max Gate was on the outskirts of the town, both the Hardys were often seen in the centre, Mrs Hardy frightening the locals by free-wheeling down the hill of the main street with her feet off her bicycle pedals, and Hardy walking in the road so that no-one brushed into him.

Lower left. Looking across the front of Max Gate in about 1886 towards the treed hump of Conquer Barrow, a big Bronze Age burial mound. Max Gate was the first house to be built in the area, and is now totally grown in with trees. Hardy's admirers were often surprised by his redbrick villa: they expected him to be in an old stone manor house. Many of these were for sale in the 1880s when the Hardys moved back to Dorchester, but he preferred this solid new house, designed by himself and built by his brother Henry's building firm.

Below. The Forum, Rome, from the Hardys' album. They travelled in Italy for six weeks in 1887, visiting Venice, Milan and Florence as well as Rome. Hardy was interested in the places associated with the English poets who had lived there – Byron, Shelley, Browning and Keats, and later wrote a poem about Keats's grave in Rome. Hardy found Rome overpowering, feeling 'its measureless layers of history to lie upon him like a physical weight'.

A rare informal photograph of Hardy, taken by his friend Gosse in September 1890 just after he had finished *Tess*. Hardy looks youngish, although he was fifty, and unconventional with his beard. He was bearded from before 1870 until about Christmas 1891, after the publication of *Tess*, in fact all the time he was writing fiction except his last novel. Removing the beard made him look much older, and such an extreme change may have been the outward result of some inner turmoil.

The back garden at Max Gate was still bare, but the masses of tiny trees soon grew to enclose it. Moss, Hardy's black retriever bitch, died soon after and Hardy asked Gosse for copies, as they were the only photographs taken of her.

Hardy in his study drawn for a magazine about 1892. This was the second room used as a study at Max Gate, and is where he wrote *Tess of the D'Urbervilles*. Journalists visiting after its publication, when he was much in the news, were surprised at his appearance and thought he looked like a Londoner, which he considered himself partly to be. In 1891 he had been made a member of the prestigious Athenaeum, one of the most important London clubs.

Right. Tess feeding sheaves to the threshing machine, an illustration from the magazine serialisation.

Lower right. Nastassia Kinski as Tess Durbeyfield and Peter Firth as Angel Clare in the milking scene from the 1979 film of *Tess of the D'Urbervilles*, 'Tess', directed by Roman Polanski for Columbia Pictures Corporation Ltd.

Thomas Hardy senior, the novelist's father photographed later in life, looking very prosperous. He died in 1892, aged 80, still in the cottage where he was born. The novelist recorded that the last thing his father asked for was water fresh from their well, and after tasting it he said 'Yes – that's our well-water. Now I know I am at home'. Hardy admired his father's simple life and constant residence at Bockhampton. Although sincerely mourned, Thomas Hardy senior's death did not alter the family's circumstances. His son Henry continued to run the building business, and his wife Jemima went on living at the cottage.

A wood engraving from the 1926 edition of *Tess*, by Vivien Gribble. Hardy suggested that Gertrude Bugler, 'the very incarnation' of Tess, should sit for some of the engravings. The illustrations are in a 'modern' style totally different from that of the originals of forty years earlier. Hardy liked both.

One of the portraits from Wool Manor, used by Hardy in *Tess of the D'Urbervilles* for some of Tess's ancestors: 'The billhook nose, large teeth, and bold eye' suggest 'arrogance to the point of ferocity', and both 'haunt the beholder afterwards in his dreams'. One small example of Hardy's use of true details.

An engraving of about 1790 showing the strange rocky landscape of Portland, the setting for Hardy's second to last novel *The Well Beloved*, photographed in 1898, soon after the novel was published. Bow and Arrow Castle (left) is just below the main street of Easton, where the cottage Hardy used as the heroines' home still survives. This strange, very separate piece of Dorset, although not truly an island but very isolated, was known to Hardy as a visitor all his life. Strangers from the mainland were not accepted by the islanders, who preserved their own ways and customs.

Hardy looking like an Alpine climber in his cycling clothes standing beside his 'Druid stone' in the garden of Max Gate in the later 1890s. This sarsen was found probably in 1890, and needed several men with levers to position it upright on the edge of the lawn. In 1987 excavations next door to Max Gate found half a Neolithic causewayed enclosure: the other half lies in Hardy's garden, surrounding the house. This stone must have been part of the Neolithic enclosure used for the disposal of the dead, which dates from about the third millenium BC.

Poetry, Emma and other Women

1895–1912

At Christmas 1890, after the furore of *Tess* Hardy thought seriously of returning to poetry and writing no more fiction, and it seems likely that he intended *Jude* to be his last book even before he wrote it. The hostile reception of that novel, published in book form in 1895, finalised the decision.

In 1896 he expalined some of his reasons for the change. 'Perhaps I can express more fully in verse ideas and emotions which run counter to the inert crystallized opinion – hard as a rock – which the vast body of men have vested interests in supporting. To cry out in a passionate poem that (for instance) the Supreme Mover or Movers must be either limited in power, unknowing, or cruel – which is obvious enough, and has been for centuries – will cause them merely a shake of the head; but to put it in argumentative prose will make them sneer, or foam, and set all the literary contortionists jumping upon me, a harmless agnostic, as if I were a clamorous atheist'.

Several times in his autobiography Hardy produces the odd idea that he didn't write 'real' novels, which he defined as 'stories of modern artificial life and manners showing a certain smartness of treatment'. What he had aimed at was 'keeping his narratives close to natural life and as near to poetry in their subject as the conditions would allow'. With his usual pessimism, he had always feared that he might be driven to writing society novels, and had kept a record of his experiences in society as background just in case. He felt great relief at giving this up.

The novels and short stories, particularly *Tess* and *Jude* had made him a rich man. He was lucky that a proper copyright law had been made law in America in December 1890, so that *Tess* and *Jude* were protected.

His first volume of poetry *Wessex Poems and other verses* was published in 1898, with his own line drawings. A third of the poems dated from the 1860s (although doubtless revised) when he was a young man working in London. Reviewers were surprised by the change, but gradually he was accepted as a poet, publishing two more volumes before 1910, as well as *The Dynasts*. Much of his poetry was first published in newspapers and magazines.

Hardy was forty-five when he gave up writing fiction, and from that time on he travelled more, both in this country and abroad as well as visiting London for the season. He thought the chief objection to a country life was the lack of good music freely available in London. Hardy liked opera, and was pleased when, in 1903, an opera based on *Tess* was written. He was amused when Vesuvius erupted simultaneously with the first performance in Naples. Cycling, then very fashionable, became a passion with both him and his wife. In 1897 they went to Switzerland at the time of the Golden Jubilee of

Queen Victoria, travelling in the opposite direction to the rest of the world coming to London for the celebrations.

In the 1890s, when he revised his novels for a collected edition, Hardy tidied up the place names so that they were the same in all of them. Simultaneously visitors started to explore 'Hardy's Wessex', and books identifying the real places were published. Hardy provided the information for several of these.

In 1903 he published the first part of *The Dynasts*, an epic verse drama of the Napoleonic wars from 1805, including the death of Nelson and scenes with Napoleon in France, the House of Commons in London, as well as local Dorset material. The whole is manipulated and commented on by spirits, and is an odd combination of unactable play and long poem. Much of it is blank (ie unrhymed) verse with prose, and songs in rhymed verse. Hardy considered it his best work, but few others have.

Jemima Hardy, his mother, died in 1904 at the age of ninety. She had lived at the Bockhampton cottage for nearly sixty-five years, looked after for the last seven or eight years by her daughters who had given up teaching.

Hardy continued being infatuated by women, especially younger women, and sometime in 1905 he met Florence Dugdale. She had trained as a teacher (like both his sisters) but was partly earning her living writing children's stories. Nearly forty years younger than Hardy, she did little research jobs for him, and by 1910 she was typing for both Thomas and Emma Hardy. Hardy helped her with her writing, and sent stories to editors for her.

Emma claimed to have written much of Hardy's fiction, and with increasing age became more aggressively Protestant and generally odd, a sad combination of childishness, naivety and age and possibly even mental disturbance. Hardy's public agnosticism upset her greatly and she wrote rather bad poetry and a strange short religious book. Most visitors found her difficult, and her habit of contradicting Hardy in public was embarrassing. However, it is easy to overemphasise their differences. In 1903 Hardy wrote to Mrs Henniker complaining that he and Emma had just read a Henry James novel, and both had enjoyed it, but discussing it afterwards they found they both had totally different ideas as to what had actually happened in the novel. This hardly represents total estrangement. Emma died suddenly in November 1912.

Above. Max Gate about 1900, with Hardy and his bicycle, and Emma standing by the roller with her nephew Gordon Gifford. He and his sister spent a lot of their childhood with the Hardys, Gordon even attending a Dorchester school for some time. By 1900 the trees around Max Gate were getting quite large. The Hardy's marriage was unhappy by this time, Hardy writing to Mrs Hennicker in 1896 that he couldn't see any possible scheme for the union of the sexes that would be satisfactory.

Top right . The drawing room at Max Gate, probably about 1900. A classic late Victorian room, with a palm in a pot, shrouded table and screen, all with quite a lot of clutter. This was where the many visitors were entertained to tea.

Right. The hall at Max Gate, probably about 1900-1910. A visitor in 1904 was surprised to have the door opened by Hardy himself rather than a servant, and astonished that he had no shoes on. Emma explained that he was not allowed to wear boots until the kittens were three weeks old, in case they were hurt.

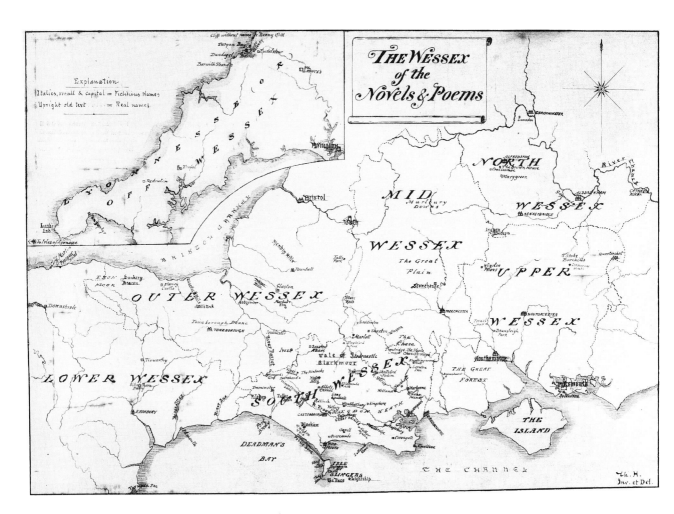

Left. Hardy's Wessex, a map drawn by the
novelist in 1895 to show all the places mentioned
in his novels, using their fictional names.
Although he always claimed that 'Wessex' was far
larger than Dorset the density of place-names
within the county shows clearly that it occurs far
more often than anywhere else.

Lower left. The White Horse Inn, Maiden Newton,
Dorset, a fine 17th century building, just the sort
of old-fashioned inn that Hardy liked to visit
while out on drives. In 1897 the owner decided he
wanted to demolish it, and Hardy went to
examine it for the Society for the Protection of
Ancient Buildings, and his report sympathised
with the owner's wanting larger rooms for visitors
and admitted the bad state of the building. Hardy
proposed a compromise whereby the exterior of
the building was preserved and the interior
modernised, but the inn was demolished in 1898.

Above and left. Budmouth (really Weymouth) and
Mellstock (Stinsford) school drawn by Edmund
New for Bertram Windle's *Thomas Hardy's Wessex*
published in 1902. Stinsford school was the first
one Hardy attended. This was one of several
books which appeared around that time
describing the settings of Hardy's fiction. He
supplied Windle with a list of the real places, but
emphasised that 'the places in the novels were
only *suggested* by the real ones – they are not
literally portraits'.

Above. The Whitefriars club, a journalists' and literary club, outside Max Gate in June 1901, with Hardy centre and Emma second from his right. The trip was called 'A pilgrimage to Wessex', and there were so many pilgrims that a tent had to be put up on the lawn for tea. Smaller garden parties were held regularly every summer from the 1890s until Emma's death in 1912.

Left. Hardy's mother Jemima in 1903, in the garden of the Bockhampton cottage. In 1901 the Whitefriars club were driven the last ten miles to Bockhampton in open carriages, and Jemima made her disapproving daughters wheel her in her chair to the road they would pass along, where she waved her handkerchief to them. They didn't know who she was. Hardy visited the cottage frequently to see his family, but Emma did not get on with them.

When Hardy moved to Max Gate he was a neighbour to William Barnes, who had lived from 1864 in the picturesque thatched rectory of Winterborne Came, a mile from Max Gate across the fields. Hardy often visited him, and wrote a fine poem about his funeral. When asked by Barnes's biographer (and daughter) what they had talked about, Hardy had to admit that they simply gossiped about people they knew.

Left. Hardy with his bicycle about 1900. He described himself as 'not a long-distance cyclist, as was natural at fifty-nine, never exceeding forty to fifty miles a day'. Mrs Hardy was also an enthuisast, and they cycled all over Dorset and even beyond, sometimes in company with friends.

Below. Talbothays, West Stafford, two miles east of Max Gate, designed by Hardy and built by his brother Henry in 1893. It was let until 1913, when Henry, Mary and Kate all came to live here, Henry from the Bockhampton cottage, Kate and Mary from their house in Dorchester.

Above. Henry Hardy was ten years younger than Thomas, Kate sixteen years younger, so that they were almost another generation from Thomas and the elder sister Mary who was born only a year after the novelist. Both the sisters were teachers, while Henry took over the family building firm. There are no photographs of Mary surviving. His family was very important to Hardy: he visited his mother at the cottage most Sundays, and after her death visited Talbothays and his brother and sisters just as frequently.

Right. Hardy's favourite sister Mary, the only certain likeness of her to survive. She painted all her family, but this self-portrait is perhaps the best.

Hardy the socialite, at Arlington Manor, Newbury during a visit to Sir Francis Jeune and his wife in 1895. Jeune was a judge who entertained Hardy with stories of the divorce courts, and his wife was a leading London hostess who introduced Hardy to many people. He was friendly with the whole family: her children by her first marriage called him Uncle Tom and remained friends all his life. None of them could stand Emma, who did however, accompany him for the visit when this photograph was taken. A. C. Benson, who disliked Max Gate and Emma, described Hardy acidly in 1912 as looking like 'a retired half-pay officer, from a not very smart regiment'.

Hardy got on far better with the people he met in London, even the aristocrats, than he did with Dorset landowners whom he felt merely tolerated him. His plebian origins and hatred of all blood sports were probably the reasons for this.

Florence Hennicker, who Hardy met in 1893 when he visited the Viceregal Lodge, Dublin. She was in her late 30s, had already published three novels, and was upper-class, beautiful and married. Hardy was immediately infatuated, and despite (or perhaps because of) Mrs Hennicker's rejection of his advances, they remained friends all her life. They collaborated on a short story, and she gave him a silver inkstand which he always kept on his desk.

Hardy with Florence Dugdale on Aldeburgh
beach in August 1909, their first visit together to
Edward Clodd. They visited him a couple of times
a year until Emma's death in 1912. Hardy was
sixty-nine, Florence thirty in 1909.

Above left. Emma Hardy late in life. Gosse described her in 1912 as 'absurdly dressed, as a country lady without friends might dress herself on a vague recollection of some nymph in a picture by Botticelli'.

Above. Florence Griffin outside Max Gate, about 1910, with one of the cats. She was Emma Hardy's maid, and stayed on as housekeeper after Emma's death. Dorchester gossips thought Florence Griffin would marry Hardy. There were normally three indoor servants at Max Gate: cook, parlour maid and another maid, besides a gardener and sometimes a page. Maids in uniform hardly accord with one's image of Hardy, but of course all middle class households had servants then.

Left. Hardy at a rehearsal of *The Mellstock Quire*, in 1910, a play adapted by the Hardy Players from *Under the Greenwood Tree*. This group of amateur actors grew out of an earlier debating society, and between 1908 and 1924 they performed seven plays from Hardy's fiction.

Drawings by William Strang of Hardy and
Florence Dugdale in 1910. Strang came to Max
Gate to draw the official portrait of Hardy as a
member of the Order of Merit, an honour he had
just received, and Hardy asked him to sketch
Florence who was then acting as his secretary. It
was Florence's favourite likeness of herself. Hardy
had refused a knighthood in 1908, but was
pleased by the award of OM, a high honour which
was limited to 24 recipients.

Emma Hardy with umbrella on Worthing beach in
July 1911, a fortnight holiday she took with
Florence Dugdale (standing). During the second
half of their marriage Emma often took holidays
alone, and had wanted Florence to go to France
with her. Apart from a few close friends, people
were supposed to think that Florence was Emma's
friend, not Hardy's, and Emma herself believed it.

Poetry, Old Age and Florence

1912–1928

Hardy was filled with remorse after Emma's death, compounded of sorrow at losing her and bitter remorse for his neglect. They had been married for nearly forty years, and after her death memories of their early happiness flooded back. Hardy defined poetry as 'emotion put into measure. The emotion must come by nature, but the measure can be acquired by art'. The emotions after Emma's death brought a flood of fine poetry, some published in *Satires of Circumstance* as 'Poems of 1912-13'. He continued to write poems about Emma for the rest of his life. The haunting poems do not ignore the later problems of the marriage. 'The Voice':

> 'Woman much missed, how you call to me,
>   call to me,
> Saying that now you are not as you were
> When first you had changed from the one
>   who was all to me,
> But as at first, when our day was fair.'

Florence Dugdale moved into Max Gate immediately after Emma's death, scandalising Dorchester gossips. Hardy soon found diaries which Emma had kept for her last twenty years detailing her grievances against him. Florence called them 'diabolical'. He burnt them, but they haunted him. Less than six months after her death he went on a pilgrimage to St Juliot, where he and Emma had met, and arranged for a memorial to her in the church. Little more than a year after Emma's death Forence and Hardy were married quietly at Enfield where her parents lived, succeeding in avoiding the publicity both were frightened of. Florence, often melancholy herself, took on a husband aged seventy-three (ten years older than her father) who was often himself melancholy. She later felt that she had slipped from youth (she was only thirty five when she maried) to 'dreary middle-age' when she moved to Max Gate, but it was her unremitting care of Hardy which enabled him to live another fourteen years and produce five more volumes of poetry.

They travelled around quite a lot during the first six months of marriage, but after that the First World War and Hardy's age led to them not even going to London for the season, as he had done all through his marriage with Emma. Hárdy worked regularly in his study each morning, telling a visitor that it was important not to wait for the right mood, because if you did it would come less and less. In the afternoons he went for a walk and entertained the many distinguished visitors who came to pay their respects to the greatest living writer. In the evening Florence read aloud. She found Max Gate lonely and the regular routine boring. Although Hardy stopped writing fiction in the 1890s, he continued to earn well from the novels. Deluxe versions like the Mellstock edition of 1919 (limited to 500 copies) sold well, as did normally priced ones. Hardy always dealt with publishers and magazine editors himself, not using an agent, and was shrewd at getting a good price, including good fees from magazines for his poetry.

Hardy described himself as being capable of 'burying an emotion in my head or brain for forty years, and exhuming it at the end of that time as fresh as when interred'. His famous poem 'In time of "The Breaking of Nations"' 'contained a feeling that moved me in 1870, during the Franco-Prussian War' when he was in Cornwall, but not written until 1915:

> 'Only a man harrowing clods
>   In a slow silent walk
> With an old horse that stumbles and nods
>   Half asleep as they stalk.
>
> Only thin smoke within flame
>   From the heaps of couch-grass;
> Yet this will go onward the same
>   Though Dynasties pass.
>
> Yonder a maid and her wight
>   Come whispering by:
> War's annals will cloud into night
>   Ere their story die.'

The Boer War (1899-1902) had made Hardy realise that the romance he had seen in earlier wars was gone, but the First World War 'destroyed all [his] belief in the gradual ennoblement of man, a belief he had held for many years'. Until the First World War Hardy had described himself as a meliorist, a word coined in the mid 19th century to describe a state between optimism and pessimism, which included the belief that human efforts could make the world better. Most of Hardy's friends thought he was always a pessimist, and even before the War he wrote a letter 'Pessimism – as the optimists nickname what is really only a reasoned view of effects and probable causes, deduced from facts un-flinchingly observed – leads to a mental quietude that tends rather upwards than downwards'. Summarised in the poem 'In Tenebris II', 'if way to the Better there be, it extracts a full look at the Worst'. Amid the carnage the distant cousin Hardy hoped would be his heir was killed.

Many of Hardy's poems during the war and after are very bitter:

> Christmas: 1924
> '"Peace upon earth!" was said. We sing it,
> And pay a million priests to bring it.
> After two thousand years of mass
> We've got as far as poison-gas'

Despite being widely seen as England's greatest living writer, Hardy was still overly sensitive to any criticism of his poetry or prose and his bitterness towards critics suprised many people. He was friendly with many younger writers, especially poets, and was very touched by the 'poets' tribute' which Siegfried Sassoon organised for Hardy's seventy-ninth birthday – a volume in which forty-three poets had each written out one of their poems.

Hardy hated details of his personal life being published, claiming that the less readers knew about an author in his lifetime the better, and to forestall biographies being written after he was dead, he wrote his autobiography in the third person (referring to himself as Mr Hardy, rather than I), intending that it should be published posthumously, then giving Florence as the author. They worked on it during 1917-1919, with Hardy destroying the diaries and other private papers as he used them.

Hardy became ill in December 1927, at first seemingly not seriously, but he took permanently to his bed on Christmas day and died on 11 January 1928, aged eighty seven.

Above. Whitcombe, only a short distance from Max Gate, and one of Hardy's favourite walks, taken in 1912. In this tiny hamlet the barn (right) seems larger than the church (left). Hardy's friend, William Barnes the Dorset poet, was rector to both this church and nearby Winterborne Came from 1862 until his death in 1886, and Hardy had attended at least one of his services here.

Left. Hardy in the robes of the honorary degree bestowed on him by Cambridge university in June 1913. His sister Mary wrote to remind him that in the early 1860s a Cambridge degree had been his aim, so that he could become a clergyman and 'now you have accomplished it all with greater honour than if you had gone along the road you then saw before you'.

Opposite page. Florence and Thomas Hardy with the dreaded dog Wessex outside Max Gate soon after their marriage. Florence had bought the dog as a puppy in 1913, finding Max Gate isolated and needing a guard dog. Wessex lived for thirteen years being thoroughly spoilt by both the Hardys and biting everyone else, visitors (except T E Lawrence) and postmen alike. Cynthia Asquith was horrified in 1921. Wessex 'was specially uninhibited at dinner-time, most of which he spent not under but on the table, walking about unchecked, and contesting every single forkful of food on its way from my plate to my mouth'.

Christmas card of 1923, with Wessex sitting outside Max Gate waiting for someone to bite.

Hardy with his sister Kate (second left), Florence (fourth left at the back) and lots of other people in the woods at the back of the birthplace, Higher Bockhampton about 1920, perhaps for a summer day picnic. This snap from Kate's album is a reminder of Hardy's local friendships.

GREETINGS - - - from
Mr. and Mrs. THOMAS HARDY

Max Gate,
Dorchester.   Xmas. 1923

Augustus John's portrait of Hardy, painted in 1923. Although Hardy said that if he looked like that, the sooner he was underground the better, he must have mellowed towards the painting since in 1927 he said 'I don't know whether that is how I look or not, but that is how I *feel*'. T. E. Lawrence suggested that John should paint the portrait, and he certainly liked it himself and felt that both the Hardys liked it.

Left. Mr and Mrs Thomas Hardy with the Balliol players, Oxford undergraduates who included Max Gate in their tour of the west of England with a Greek play in July 1923, the first of three such visits. Hardy recorded that it was a windy day and 'the players with their bare arms and legs and scanty costumes must have been none too comfortable'. Instead of flaming torches, invisible in sunlight, 'they carried tall spikes of giant flowering spiraea which they plucked from the border'. It seems to have been a cheerful occasion, as were Hardy's two visits to Oxford in old age. In 1920 he went to see an undergraduate version of *The Dynasts* and be presented with an honorary degree. His last long journey, and the last time he slept away from Max Gate, was in 1923 when he visited Oxford to be made an honorary fellow. All this contrasts with his treatment of the fictional Oxford 'Christminster' in *Jude* written fifty years earlier.

Lower left. The Hardys with the Prince of Wales in the garden of Max Gate, 20 July 1923. The Prince and Hardy drove through the streets of Dorchester together in an open car, and then had lunch at Max Gate. Dorchester was highly impressed, and finally realised quite how famous Hardy was.

Below. Hardy in his study at Max Gate, about 1920. This was his third and last study at Max Gate, part of the additions to the house and used from the early 1890s, so that *Jude the Obscure* and much of the poetry was written here. Cynthia Asquith visited in 1921 and thought the house small scale, and the study 'the only room in the house that had any character . . . simple, bare, workmanlike and pleasantly shabby' with walls 'distempered an unusual shade of coral pink'. There is a reconstruction of this study in the Dorset County Museum, Dorchester.

Mr and Mrs Hardy with Wessex, going to vote in 1924. Hardy tried to keep out of politics, but in a letter of 1883 he described himself as a Liberal, and he was one of the Liberal sympathisers listed by the Prime Minister as potential peers if the bill limiting the powers of the House of Lords was not passed.

T. E. Lawrence, a copy of a portrait by Augustus John, sent by Lawrence to the Hardys. Hardy described Lawrence as one of his most valued friends, although they only met in 1923 when Lawrence was serving at Bovington Camp near to Dorchester and parted in 1926 when Lawrence was posted to India.

Above. Hardy in the drawing room at Max Gate in 1925, flanked by two actresses who played Tess in the Barnes Theatre Company productions, one touring, one in London. They came to Max Gate in 1924 to perform the play which was running successfully in London that year. The parlour maid remembered how 'Max Gate became alive that evening'. She and the other maid sat under the piano to see the performance. Hardy was too frail to go to London to see the production, and so it was brought to Max Gate.

Right. Hardy explaining Tess to Gwen Ffangcon-Davies in 1925 with Florence (right). Ffangcon-Davies was to star in the London production that year. Gertrude Bugler had been offered the part, but Florence Hardy, hysterical about Hardy's infatuation with the beautiful girl, begged her not to take it. Gertrude Bugler was unaware of Hardy's feelings: he was old enough to be her grandfather.

Hardy and Gosse in the garden of Max Gate, June 1927, with Cobweb, Hardy's cat. Gosse wrote Hardy 'is a wonder if you like! At 87½ without a deficiency of sight, hearing, mind or conversation. Very tiny and fragile, but full of spirit and gaiety not quite consistent in the most pessimistic of poets. He and I collogued merrily of past generations like two antediluvian animals sporting in the primaeval slime'.

Hardy and Gosse were friends for 53 years; both were dead within a year of this photograph being taken.

Hardy making a rare speech at the laying of the foundation stone of new buildings for Dorchester Grammar School in July 1927. His speech was mostly about the Elizabethan Thomas Hardy who founded the school. The occasion tired him (he looks very old and frail in the photograph) and when he got home he said that he had made his last public appearance, which was true.

Looking east from Bulbarrow with the vale of
Blackmoor beyond. In the 1920s Hardy hired a car
and driver a couple of times a week in summer, to
take him and Florence on trips around Dorset.
Even in old age he was still exploring the county,
and preferred to go inland rather than visit the
coast. The hired car was an open one, and Hardy
would not allow the driver to exceed twenty-five
miles an hour.

Hardy often walked across the river valley from Max Gate to Stinsford church to tend the family graves. The cottage at Bockhampton, Stinsford church and the big house at Kingston Maurwood had been the important places of his youth, and they remained important in his old age. Hardy's low gravestone is just visible behind the upright gravestones in the left foreground.

Eva Dugdale, one of Florence's four sisters, in her nurse's uniform about 1910. She got on well with Hardy, and nursed him during an illness in 1922. Although Hardy's letters are full of complaints about minor illnesses – London always gives him influenza, he has a 'watery eye' or rheumatism – he was really very healthy. In 1927, when he fell ill with a chill Eva came to help her sister again. Hardy's last words were to her: "Eva, Eva, what is this?"

Afterwards

Hardy's will indicated that he was to be buried at Stinsford, in the churchyard he had thought of as the most holy place on earth, full of memories of his first wife, his parents and earlier ancestors. Sidney Cockerell, his joint literary executor (with Florence) and James Barrie decided otherwise and applied to have Hardy buried in Poet's Corner, Wesminster Abbey. Hardy's brother and sister were horrified, especially as he had to be cremated: 'a staggering blow' was how Kate described it. The compromise finally reached was gruesome: Hardy's heart was removed for burial at Stinsford, and after cremation at Woking his ashes were buried at Westminster. The two funerals were simultaneous on 16 January 1928, Florence and Kate going to the one in London, and his brother Henry to Stinsford. Florence later regretted being persuaded into the dual burial. A local comment was 'And when the Day of Judgement be come, Almighty, e'll say: 'Ere be 'eart, but where be rest of 'e".

Hardy left an estate valued at £90,000, in modern terms more than two million pounds, which surprised local people who knew how mean he had been. In the middle 1920s Hardy had been earning £5,000 a year or more, when a doctor's average yearly wage was £756, a miner or London bus driver earnt £190 and an agricultural labourer £82. Florence was left an annuity of £600 a year and all the royalties from his books. Since Hardy continued to be a popular author, the royalties were substantial. Florence improved Max Gate, bought a car and employed a chauffeur and rented a flat in London. These were all things she had wanted to do in Hardy's lifetime.

As soon as he was dead, there were innumerable suggestions of a physical memorial to Hardy. Cockerell wanted a huge tower, and Augustus John thought a statue on Egdon Heath would be 'more symbolical'. The memorial committee with Florence finally decided on a life-sized statue in Dorchester, which was unveiled in 1931 by Hardy's friend James Barrie.

The first volume of Hardy's autobiography, issued as being by Florence, was published in 1928, and the second in 1930. Both were well received. Florence lived only ten years after Hardy's death, dying in 1937 of cancer, aged fifty eight. During her short widowhood she did much good work for the local hospital, and for the Mill Street Housing Society, which cleared and improved the slums of Fordington, a suburb of Dorchester Hardy had described in *The Mayor of Casterbridge*.

Hardy's birthplace at Bockhampton was acquired by the National Trust in 1948, and preserved as a memorial to him. The Society for the Protection of Ancient Buldings sold Hardy's letter to them and other manuscripts in 1930 for £1,000 using the money to restore the simple Norman church at Winterborne Tomson, fifteen miles east of Dorchester.

Hardy's real memorial, of course, is his fiction and poetry. Both have continued to be popular since his death, and many books and articles on the man and his works have been published, and continue to be published. A bibliography listing articles and books about Hardy or his works has more than 3,000 entries for 1961-1968, but there were 1,316 more published in 1970-1978, and doubtless many more than that in the last ten years. There is a Thomas Hardy Society in England and another in Japan. The novels continue to be translated, and turned into films – there were five made in Hardy's lifetime, all silent.

Special.

WESTMINSTER ABBEY.

——

FUNERAL OF
THE LATE THOMAS HARDY, O.M.

——

MONDAY, 16TH JANUARY, 1928, AT 2 P.M.

ADMIT BEARER
TO SOUTH TRANSEPT.

ADMISSION BY POETS' CORNER,
VIA OLD PALACE YARD,
BEFORE 1.45 P.M.

W. FOXLEY NORRIS,
DEAN.

A ticket for Hardy's funeral in Westminster Abbey. It is difficult to know whether Hardy would have approved of his being buried there. He accepted many honours, and he urged memorials for other poets such as Byron to be placed in the Abbey. After the memorial service for the novelist George Meredith (who had been refused burial in the Abbey) Hardy suggested a heathen annexe 'strictly accursed by the Dean and clergy on its opening day' to hold authors who were not Christian.

The funeral at Stinsford. Four years earlier Hardy had written to the vicar of Stinsford 'regard me as a Parishioner certainly. I hope to be still more one when I am in a supine position some day'. He had described Tennyson's burial in Westminster Abbey in 1892 as 'less impressive than a plain country interment would have been'. Clearly Hardy intended to be buried at Stinsford, but as an antiquarian he might have been pleased by the heart burial because it was a medieval practice for important people.

BUSTS OF

Thomas Hardy, O.M.,

— IN DORSET WARE —

(Produced by Permission).

J. T. GODWIN, . . .

 10, HIGH WEST STREET,

DORCHESTER,

Has secured the first Consignment.

Price 3/6 each. **10 inches high.**

Post Free.

Little ceramic busts of Hardy offered by the local china merchant after the award of the Order of Merit in 1910 made Dorchester realise just how famous he was. Hardy found it difficult to cope with fame: he was a shy man in public and hated anyone touching him. It was probably the floods of visitors to Thomas Hardy's Wessex who bought these busts, as he was not generally popular locally.

Left. Eric Kennington working on the memorial statue. T. E. Lawrence admired the finished statue: 'It holds somehow that strange effect of living within himself that always Hardy gave me . . . the figure will be beautiful as well as a memorial'.

Right. Sir James Barrie unveiling the Hardy Memorial in September 1931. Hardy and Barrie had been friends since the 1890s, and Barrie came to Max Gate during Hardy's last illness to help Florence.

Below. Crowds at the statue on 2 June 1940, the 100th anniversary of Hardy's birth, which coincided with the evacuation of the British Army from Dunkirk, completed only two days later. Despite the War, the centenary was celebrated by exhibitions, articles in the national press, and two services at Stinsford church with early 19th century church music, besides the laying of a wreath at the statue seen here.

Below. When Florence Hardy died, only nine years after her husband, she left the contents of his study (and much manuscript material) to the Dorset County Museum, Dorchester where the study was re-created. Kate Hardy, the novelist's surviving sister is seen here cutting the ceremonial ribbon. John Masefield, Poet Laureate, assisted at the opening.

Right. Two photographs of Hardy's last study, reconstructed in the Dorset County Museum, Dorchester, with the original furniture from Max Gate left to the museum by his widow, Florence. It is smaller than the original room. Above the fireplace are framed illustrations from *Jude*. On his desk are the things he kept there, including the silver inkstand (left of stationery box) given to him in 1893 by Florence Hennicker. After his first wife Emma died in 1912 he kept his calendar at 7th March to commemorate the day me met her in 1870.

Covers from *The Mayor of Casterbridge* translated
into Tamil (left, probably 1960s) and the same
novel in Hungarian, 1968 (right). Hardy's novels
were translated into French from the 1880s,
followed by other European languages. He was
particularly friendly with one of his French
translators, helping her with dialect words and
others like 'lynchets' which were difficult. Hardy
is now one of the most translated novelists, his
works appearing in Russian, Japanese, and many
Indian languages as well as all European ones.

Right. Bathsheba Everdene and Gabriel Oak from
the 1915 silent film of *Far From the Madding Crowd,*
the second of Hardy's novels to be filmed: *Tess* was
the first.

Bathsheba Everdene (Julie Christie) and Gabriel
Oak (Alan Bates) in the 1967 film of *Far from the
Madding Crowd*.

Tess and her baby in the cornfield, a striking
image from the 1979 film starring Nastassia
Kinski. Today more people probably know
Hardy's novels from films or television than from
the printed page.

Chronology

1840 Born on June 2nd at Higher Bockhampton, first child of Thomas and Jemima Hardy.
1850 Goes to school in Dorchester.
1856 Articled to John Hicks, architect of Dorchester.
1862 Moves to London.
1867 Returns to Dorset.
1867 Starts *The Poor Man and the Lady*, which is rejected by publishers.
1870 Meets Emma Gifford at St Juliot, Cornwall.
1871 *Desperate Remedies* published.
1872 *Under the Greenwood Tree* published.
1872 Gives up architecture and becomes a writer full-time.
1873 *A Pair of Blue Eyes* published.
1874 Marries Emma Gifford, and *Far from the Madding Crowd* published.
1875 Moves from London to Swanage, then Yeovil, in early 1876.
1876 Moves to Sturminster Newton: *The Hand of Ethelberta* published.
1878 Moves to Tooting, and *The Return of the Native* published.
1880 *The Trumpet Major* published.
1881 Moves to Wimborne, and *A Laodicean* published.
1882 *Two on a Tower* published.
1883 Moves back to Dorchester.
1885 Moves into Max Gate.
1886 *The Mayor of Casterbridge* published.

1887 *The Woodlanders* published.
1888 *Wessex Tales* (short stories) published.
1891 *A Group of Noble Dames* (short stories) and *Tess of the D'Urbervilles* published.
1892 *The Well-Beloved* published as a serial, book publication 1897.
1894 *Life's Little Ironies* (short stories) published.
1895 *Jude the Obscure* published.
1898 *Wessex Poems*, his first volume of poetry, published.
1901 *Poems of the Past and Present* published.
1904 First of three parts of *The Dynasts*, his epic verse drama, published.
1909 *Time's Laughingstocks* (poetry) published.
1912 Emma Hardy dies.
1913 *A Changed Man and other Tales* published. Hermann Lea's *Thomas Hardy's Wessex* published.
1914 Marries Florence Dugdale, and *Satires of Circumstance* (poetry) published.
1917 *Moments of Vision* (poetry) published.
1922 *Late Lyrics and Earlier* (poetry) published.
1923 *The Famous Tragedy of the Queen of Cornwall* published.
1925 *Human Shows, Far Phantasies, Songs, and Trifles* (poetry) published.
1928 Dies at Max Gate on January 11th, aged 87, and his last volume of poetry – *Winter Words* – published in October.

Books about Hardy

The earliest biography was *The Life of Thomas Hardy* published in two volumes in 1928 and 1930, purporting to be by Hardy's second wife Florence, but really mostly by the novelist himself. A patchy book, parts of which are fascinating: his childhood and early days in London, or the many stories his parents and grandmother told him, but other parts dull, with long lists of social engagements.

Edmund Blunden's *Thomas Hardy* (1942) is a good summary account of Hardy's life, including many interesting quotations from contemporary reviews of Hardy's writings. Evelyn Hardy's (no relation) *Thomas Hardy. A Critical Biography* (1954) produced new ideas about influences in Hardy's life.

There are two recent biographies. Robert Gittings *Young Thomas Hardy* (1975) and *The Older Hardy* (1978) were disliked by many Hardy fans because they appeared to denigrate Hardy, but they contained much new material and are particularly interesting about Hardy the poet. Michael Millgate's *Thomas Hardy A Biography* (1982) is the standard biography, a detailed but very accessible account. There are short biographies of both Hardy's wives: *The First Mrs Thomas Hardy* by Denys King-Robinson (1979) and *The Second Mrs Hardy* (1979) by Robert Gittings and Jo Manton.

All Hardy's surviving letters have been published in seven volumes: *The Collected Letters of Thomas Hardy* edited by Richard Little Purdy and Michael Millgate. A single volume of selected letters is also available.

HE NEVER EXPECTED MUCH
[OR]
A CONSIDERATION

[A reflection] on my eighty-sixth birthday

Well, World, you have kept faith with me,
   Kept faith with me;
Upon the whole you have proved to be
   Much as you said you were.
Since as a child I used to lie
upon the leaze and watch the sky,
Never, I own, expected I
   That life would be all fair.

'Twas then you said, and since have said,
   Times since, have said,
In that mysterious voice you shed
   From clouds and hills around:
"Many have loved me desperately,
Many with smooth serenity,
While some have shown contempt for me
   Till they dropped underground.

"I do not promise overmuch,
   Child; overmuch;
Just neutral-tinted haps and such,"
   You said to minds like mine.
Wise warning for your credit's sake!
Which I for one failed not to take,
And hence could stem such strain and ache
   As each year might assign.